AS THE SNOW DRIFTS

AS THE SNOW DRIFTS

A Cozy Winter Anthology

Edited by Nicole Frail

www.andyoupress.com

Arrangement copyright © 2024 by Nicole Frail

"Third Friday" copyright © 2024 by Sarah Dawson Powell; "Cows and Kisses" copyright © 2024 by J.E. Smith; "Sunbeam" copyright © 2024 by Guihan Larsen; "A Prairie Tale" copyright © 2024 by Amy Kelly; "Revelations in the Snow" copyright © 2024 by Debby Meltzer Quick; "Winter Escape" copyright © 2024 by Eliza Vaccaro; "Snowflakes and Second Chances" copyright © 2024 by Krista Renee; "The Winter Games of Sophie Berlin" copyright © 2024 by Renata Illustrata; "Once Upon a Storm" copyright © 2024 by S.B. Rizk

This book is a work of fiction. Any references to historical events, real people, or real locales are used fictitiously. Other names, characters, places, and incidents are products of the author's imagination, and any resemblance to actual events or locales or persons, living or dead, is entirely coincidental.

All rights reserved. No part of this publication may be reproduced, distributed, or transmitted in any form or by any means, including photocopying, recording, or other electronic or mechanical methods, without the prior written permission of the publisher, except in the case of brief quotations embodied in critical reviews and certain other noncommercial uses permitted by copyright law.

For permission requests, publicity requests, or other inquiries, write to nicolefrailbooks@gmail.com.

To order in bulk or to sell this book in your retail brick-and-mortar or online store, contact nicolefrailbooks@gmail.com.

Cover design and interior illustrations by Kerri Odell
Edited and typeset by Nicole Frail/Nicole Frail Edits, LLC.

First publication: November 2024

www.nicolefrailbooks.com | @nicolefrailbooks | www.andyoupress.com | @andyoupress

Print ISBN:978-1-965852-02-6
Also available as an ebook.

"Winter is the time for comfort, for good food and warmth, for the touch of a friendly hand, and for a talk beside the fire: it is time for home."

–Edith Sitwell

Contents

Introduction   1
by Nicole Frail

"Third Friday"   3
by Sarah Dawson Powell

Sophia struggles to maintain a project she designed with her children years ago to help the less fortunate. A piece of mail with no return address could change everything for so many.

"Cows & Kisses"   23
by T.E. Smith

Lifelong friends Maggie and Ben learn that it only takes one snowy day on the ranch—and one unplanned overnight with a single camp pack—to see that love has been in front of them this whole time.

"Sunbeam"   49
by Guihan Larsen

A story about an older brother's departure for the Vietnam War, a reflection on family, Chicago winters, and the lasting weight of absence.

"Prairie Tale" 61
by *Amy Kelly*

The perils of a winter storm and the icy grips of a snow queen threaten Mary while she fetches water for her laboring Mama.

"Revelations in the Snow" 73
by *Debby Meltzer Quick*

Peter left his family four years ago, fearing that his secret could destroy them. But this winter, he's come back home, and he must decide if he should ring that bell and reveal all.

"Winter Escape" 87
by *Eliza Vaccaro*

Abby and Raven escape to a seaside resort town for a little mid-winter R&R. Romance is in the air for Abby, but after a recent breakup, she is reluctant to start anew. But the innkeeper, Jake, is just so charming...

"Snowflakes & Second Chances" 105
by *Krista Renee*

Winter, mothers, and pie. Oh, my! When a winter storm unexpectedly hits east Texas, Lulu and Ella make the most of it. . . . Turns out they aren't the only ones keeping warm.

"The Winter Games of Sophie Berlin" 121
by Renata Illustrata

Self-reliant coach Sophie Berlin believes tennis is the love of her life, but when she hosts a charity tournament over winter break, can one desirable umpire call out her need to believe in love again and change how Sophie plays the game forever?

"Once Upon a Storm" 171
by S.B. Rizk

Luna volunteers to host her family's annual Icicle Inn-Cursion, despite the potential issue of meddlesome books and creatures that live in her enchanted library. What happens when you put a family with secrets and pent-up resentment under one roof, call it a vacation, and mix in a bit of mischief caused by books who have personalities of their own?

Contributors' Library 208

About the Editor 209

Acknowledgments 210

Introduction
Nicole Frail

Thank you for selecting *As the Snow Drifts: A Cozy Winter Anthology*! This is the first title to launch from a new (super-small) independent press, and it includes the first published works of many of its contributors, so the fact that you're taking a chance on so many new voices is admirable, and we all thank you for the support you've already shown us.

Within these pages, you will find winter weather in many of its expected forms: snowflakes and snow flurries, ice and frost, below-freezing temperatures and bitter winds.

You will also come across the more common ways we seek warmth when we encounter these frigid temperatures during the winter months: designated spots on the couch and claimed blankets, hot cocoa and tea (and coffee!), lit fireplaces and firepits, and warm hugs from those we love most.

The short stories presented in this collection define the idea of *cozy* in different ways, however. When you think of being cozy, you may envision yourself wrapped in a blanket, snuggled up in front of a fire, with a warm mug of your favorite beverage and a book in your lap (and perhaps a cat or two). The storm may be raging outside, but you're inside, comforted by the idea that you and your loved ones are safe.

In *As the Snow Drifts*, seasoned and first-time authors alike certainly don't skimp on those warm-blanket and hot-chocolate moments, but they also give you weekend getaways with best friends, family reunions in enchanted houses, emotional healing through family recipes and memories, crushes that make even frozen hearts melt, that fuzzy feeling that comes with doing something selfless for neighbors and community members, and the satisfaction in knowing you've put yourself—your happiness, or literally your life—on the line for your loved ones and that they've been blessed with health and happiness in return.

We hope you enjoy our winter short story collection. *Stay safe and warm!*

THIRD FRIDAY

Third Friday

Sarah Dawson Powell

I PULL THE VAN UP to the curb and put it in park. It's a bristly twenty-five degrees outside this evening, and my two youngest were not at all enthused about spending Christmas Eve this way. If we're being honest, I'm not too happy about it either. Our family has long-standing traditions on this day aging back to when I was a child. Being here meant we didn't get to carry out our usual traditions.

But it's the third Friday of the month, and come rain, snow, or shine, this is what we do on the third Friday of every month.

"Hats and gloves," I remind the kids. "You're gonna need them."

"Huh?" Holden asks, barely glancing up from his iPhone.

Leilani rolls her eyes. "Put your phone down and listen, dipwad."

"Stop," I tell her as she opens the passenger door. "C'mon, Holden. Let's get set up."

Holden is only ten, but he's been helping out since he was eight. He knows the drill. Leilani is fifteen and entirely tired of her brother's existence.

Stepping out of the van, I'm careful to avoid the slush pile that's accumulated. As cold as it is, the last thing I need is frozen toes all evening. I join Leilani at the hatch just as she opens it. Together, we pull out the first table and set it up on the sidewalk. When we go back for the second table, Holden is still sitting in the van, his phone inches from his face.

"Holden! Move it or you won't see that phone for a week."

"It's too cold for this. Can't we do it another day?"

Leilani pulls the table toward her. "Another day won't be the third Friday, so obviously not."

"Plus," I add, "we will be extra appreciated because it's so cold."

Holden finally pulls himself from the van—without gloves—just as Leilani and I are unfolding the second table. "This sucks."

"Your attitude is what sucks. Now, put some gloves on and start getting the totes out."

He lets out a grunt as he turns and snatches his gloves off the seat. "If I get frostbite, it's your fault."

"Maybe, but you're still helping."

Leilani and I start unpacking the cups and lids, the snacks we have available, and then the three coffee urns. Regular, decaf, and hot water. We have positioned the packets of hot chocolate and apple cider behind us in the van ever since the time we had someone grab the whole box of hot chocolate from the table and run.

It was about four years ago. My older daughter, Celeste, and I were manning—or womaning, as the case may be—the hot beverage table. Celeste was filling up a cup, listening to a woman talk about how she had been able to see her new grandbaby recently. I turned around to grab a few hotdogs wrapped in foil from the warmer. When I heard the stuttered grunt of disbelief spurt from Celeste's throat and the woman stop talking about the rosy cheeks of her grandchild, I turned around.

Celeste was staring down the road to the west. "That dude just made off with the hot chocolate."

A few of our usuals had yelled out for the man to stop, come back. Some shouted expletives. When I looked down at the table, I realized he had taken *all* the hot chocolate packs. The worst part was that I had just opened the fifty pack about ten minutes before it happened, and it had been the last of the hot chocolate we'd had with us. Everyone was stunned by what happened. No one was upset, just somewhat disappointed at the unexpected loss of the hot chocolate for the night. There were plenty of other hot drinks to go around.

I leave Leilani to finish setting the table and go over to help Holden pull the lids off the totes, which are nowhere near as full as they used to be. Together we set out a few pairs of gloves, some stocking caps and scarves, rolled fleece blankets, and pairs of socks. We leave more in the totes, and as people take what they need from the table, we will retrieve more from the totes. Sometimes people ask if we have a specific color, and we'll dig in the totes to see if we can meet their request.

When you have so little that you rely on handouts to keep you warm, the least you can ask for is your favorite color, and I think that wish should be granted. I don't mean to sound ungrateful, but I hate when we receive donations from people who would just buy up fifty pairs of black stretch gloves. The black stretch gloves always went quickly, some people not afraid to ask for more than one pair for extra warmth, but what I love are the donations of colored or patterned items. Items that had personality to them.

Just because a person is unhoused doesn't mean they don't enjoy pretty things. I've seen faces light up like the sun when they're handed a purple scarf or a blanket with cats on it.

It's the little things.

"Sophia," a familiar voice calls out. "We weren't sure you would come tonight, being Christmas Eve and all."

"See, Mom? Even he knows we're supposed to be at home," Holden says.

"Now, Ernest, how could we call ourselves Third Friday if we weren't here on the third Friday every month?"

Ernest makes his way to the table. His nose and cheeks are bright red from the cold and possibly from years of alcoholism, but that's not my business. What *is* my business is the hole in his stocking hat. "What you got to eat tonight? Anything hot?"

I glance over my shoulder at the tote of nonperishable food. "Just the drinks are hot tonight," I tell him. "We have granola bars, cracker packs, some beef jerky, nuts, cookies."

Ernest frowns when I turn back around. "I can't hardly eat that stuff without no teeth," he says. "Beef jerky?" He shakes his head. "What kind of cookies?"

Grabbing some fig cookies and chewy chocolate chip, I ask, "Either of these catch your fancy?" He nods as Sally and Bob walk up. "Hey, guys! How are you?" Ernest takes both packs of cookies. "Don't forget to grab you a new hat, Ernest," I tell him as Leilani hands him a cup of hot coffee.

"Can you believe what is going on around here?" Sally asks. "They're really pushing my buttons, you know." She juts a finger at me. "They think we don't know what they're up to." Nodding enthusiastically, she adds, "Just wait and see." Her head bobs a moment longer before she drops her hand. "Is there hot chocolate?"

Leilani loves Sally. When she first started coming around, she was a little scary. But we know now that she is all bark and no bite with a touch of mental illness. Sometimes she presents like she's a child or talks to us like we're her family members. Years ago, she stole ten-year-old Leilani's heart when she asked her how her kids were doing and rambled about how they must be getting so big. After Sally left that night, Leilani approached me.

"So, is she just, like, crazy or something? Why would she think I have kids?"

It was a busy evening, so my quick response was, "Not everyone's mind works the same." Later on, when we were home, Leilani and I talked more about mental illness and possible diagnoses she could have, and that despite whatever her issues were, she was human.

"How are you, Sally?" Leilani asks her tonight while adding the hot chocolate packet to the hot water. "Staying warm?"

"It's cold," Sally tells her. "It's a cold night."

Bob speaks up beside her. "January first me and Sally are moving into the high-rise over on Tenth Street. We been waiting for almost two years to get in there."

My heart leaps with joy for them. "That's so wonderful!"

"We even have some furniture donations lined up." He smiles as he takes the coffee Leilani is handing him. "It's the best Christmas gift ever."

"Mom," Holden calls out. "Where are the coats?"

I go over to where my son is standing behind the van. "All we have left are these size smalls." A quick glance at the woman at the table tells me she is not fitting into a small. "I'm so sorry. I know the Mission over on Blackstone has coats sometimes."

She sighs. "I've been there. They never have any in my size." Lifting her arms, she looks down around her. "I'm layered up, but sometimes I just wish I had a coat."

"Do you have a phone number?" I ask. "I can check with some of my resources and see if I can come up with one."

"No, no phone. It's okay." She glances down at the assortment of goods on the table. "It's okay."

"What happened to all those coats we used to get from that school, Mom?" Leilani asks.

"St. Peters? They closed down."

"Really?" a man asks. "I went there when I was a kid." He's older, with graying hair sticking out around the edges of his Vietnam Veteran baseball cap. The skin on his face is weathered, fine lines accentuating his mouth likely due to years of smoking.

"Yeah, enrollment had really declined in the last few years, I guess."

"It's the dang economy! No one can afford a good education for their kids anymore."

I laughed lightly. "Well, they can still get a good education in the public schools."

The man chortles. "Where do you think all the thugs and criminals are coming from? The public schools!"

Ignoring his statements, I ask him if he'd like a warm drink.

He takes a hot coffee. "Got any creamer?"

"There's cream and sugar on the other side of my daughter," I tell him.

"This ain't creamer." He picks up the square packets of powdered creamer. "This is crap. Do you put this in your coffee at home?"

"Sir, I don't believe we've met," I say. "My name is Sophia Patterson, and these are my kids, Leilani and Holden. Third Friday is a nonprofit organization run completely by me and my children that relies solely on donations from the community. As you already pointed out, our economy is in crisis and therefore donations are on the decline. Without some type of miracle, this is probably one of the last times we will be out here providing things at no cost to anyone who walks up. So, you can either take the powdered creamer or leave it for someone else. Completely up to you. We can only afford to purchase what the donations allow us to."

My daughter Celeste walks up with her boyfriend Kellen, the sound of snow crunching under their boots, her eyes on the man with the creamer packet in his hand. "Crazy to think that all this started as a project for Girl Scouts all those years ago." She turns to me with a smile. "Sorry we're late. Kell had to work a little extra tonight."

"They used to hand out hotdogs and books and goodie bags," Ernest tells Creamer Man. "Tons of water in the summer. Popsicles. Coats in the winter." He looks at me affectionately. "Just Sophia and her kids doing it all on their own."

I smile gratefully. "It's a labor of love."

Creamer Man is opening his creamer now. "Guess it's better than nothing."

I spot Holden sitting on the back of the van with his phone in his face again.

"Hey," a man says from off to the side, catching my attention before I can say anything to Holden. "Is this the Third Friday van?" He's looking right at Celeste.

"It is," she tells him.

His eyes dart around before he takes a few steps closer to her. She leans forward when he does, the table between them. The man whispers something to Celeste. She nods and turns around to look in the van.

I watch as she grabs a zipper sealed bag of feminine hygiene products. She's about to turn around and hand them to the man, but then she pauses, grabs a fleece blanket, and folds the baggie inside of it. When she turns around with the blanket, a rush of relief spreads across the man's face. "Grab a warm drink and some snacks, too."

"Thank you so much," he says, emotion etched across his face like he might cry.

This is why we do this. For the person who needs menstrual pads, for the man who needs to complain about the economy and subpar creamer, for the woman who's not quite in touch with reality.

For nearly fifteen years, ever since Celeste was a Brownie-level Girl Scout, this is how my family has spent the third Friday of each month. We flourished for years, thriving with donations. Now we can barely afford the coffee and snacks we hand out. Schools and businesses used to hold drives to collect items for us to give out. Churches held special collections for us. Unfortunately, it seems like it's all going to end soon.

On Tuesday evening the following week, it's especially frigid outside with an ice storm warning putting me on edge with worry over potential power outages. I make myself a cup of hot tea after starting a small fire in the fireplace.

"Keep those phones on their chargers in case the power goes out," I holler upstairs to Holden and Leilani. I wait a moment for an acknowledgment that never comes before sitting on the sofa, pulling my favorite fleece blanket over my lap. The blanket is pale blue with penguins and snowflakes, but I use it year-round because no other blanket in the house matches the softness of this one. The kids all know it's my favorite and they call it "Mom's blanket."

My mug of tea warms my cold hands as I gaze out the window into the night. In the orb around the streetlights, I can see the sleet falling quickly from the sky and hear the wind whipping the branches of the tall trees. A chill courses through me, and I look away from the fright outside and to the fire, basking in the warmth of it on my skin as I take a sip of my apple cinnamon tea.

Winter is my second favorite season, autumn being number one. I have the privilege of working from home most days. Whenever the weather is unfavorable, I am safe and warm inside my home, under my favorite blanket. Generally, I plan leaving my house in the winter based on the weather. Winter is nice when you can sit back and watch it from behind a window with a fire roaring to keep you warm.

I hear one of the kids thundering down the stairs before Leilani appears.

"You made a fire?" she asks.

"Seems like a good night for one."

She grabs a heavy knitted blanket from the basket beside the sofa. "I hope the power doesn't go out."

"Me too." I set down my tea, steam still billowing from my mug, and pick up the stack of mail I'd grabbed at the post office earlier. It's the mail for Third Friday. When I made it an official charity organization, I had to get a post office box. I only check it once or twice a month because the bulk of what we get is catalogs and advertisements for services we don't need, even if we could afford them. "We have enough firewood though, so no worries."

Grunting, she tucks the blanket under her feet. "Until our phones die."

I chuckle as I thumb through the mail. "Why don't you put it down and choose a movie we can watch?"

Leilani grabs the remote control as I spot a hand-addressed envelope made out to Third Friday with no return address. The envelope is square, as if it were a greeting card, but just by holding it, I can tell a card is not inside.

"I'm so burnt out on Christmas movies," my daughter says. "Oh! What about this one?"

Whatever is in the envelope is small and rectangular. Slipping my finger under the edge of the flap, I glance up at the TV to see the trailer for a romcom Leilani is considering. "That looks cute," I tell her.

My eyes shift downward when I get the envelope open. Carefully, I spread it open and find a scratch-off lottery ticket with a yellow Post-It note stuck to it. *Thought you could use this. Keep it up.*

I peel the yellow square of sticky paper away from the lottery card. It's red with the words *Winner Wonderland* in big green and white letters across the top. The card has already been scratched off. Confused, I frown. Why would someone send us a scratched-off lottery ticket?

Unless . . .

Quickly, I read the instructions on the card. *Reveal a snowflake, win the prize shown. Reveal a snowman, win triple the prize shown.* My eyes scan the card frantically.

I let out a gasp, and Leilani looks at me. "What?"

I can't pull my eyes from the number next to the snowman even when they blur with tears, multiplying it by three over and over, questioning the math I learned in elementary school.

"Mom?" She leans closer to see what's in my hand. "Did you win?"

Unable to speak, I hold the card out for her to take. Her green eyes study the card for a moment before they light up. "Oh, my goodness!" She looks at me. "We're definitely going on a cruise for my birthday now!" Her laugh is musical with joy.

I shake my head, searching my lap for the envelope the lottery card came in. "It's not for us."

Leilani sucks in a breath when she sees it addressed to Third Friday. "No way." Her words and expression don't give away if she's in awe or disappointed.

My tears have overflowed onto my cheeks as my mind swirls with all that I can do with the money. All *we* can do with the money.

"Mom," she says. "We can get coats, and have hotdogs again, and help Bob and Sally with things for their apartment." Sitting tall, she flaps her hand in excitement. "We can help so many people, Mom!"

The lump in my throat makes it so I can't speak, so I nod in agreement.

Leilani picks up her phone and takes a picture of the scratch-off ticket. "I'm sending it to Celeste."

I find my voice. "Send it to Dominic and Jameson, too."

Dominic is my oldest, married and living out of state. Earlier this year, Jameson, my middle child, moved in with Dom and Dom' wife, Serena, to give life a try in a new city. They were both big helps with Third Friday when it was in its prime. When I recently told Dom I was likely going to have to put an end to it, he was sad. It had been part of our family for so long.

"I sent it in the family chat," Leilani says as my phone vibrates on the end table beside me. "Just the pic," she says with a smile. "Let their minds run away like mine did for a minute."

Jameson is the first to reply. "For real or did you steal this from the Internet?"

Leilani holds the ticket next to her face and smiles as she snaps another picture. We wait for a reply.

Celeste: Wait, really?

Jameson: Let me get some lol

Dominic: You're not even old enough to buy lottery tickets lol

Celeste: So where we going first?

Jameson: Tell Mom to give me money for new tires

I pick up my phone and snap a picture of the envelope and send it in the group chat. Once it delivers, I watch the screen for their replies. There's nothing for a moment, and then Dominic says, "We need an explanation."

I type out how the card arrived in the envelope, already scratched off, with a Post-It note attached.

Dominic: That's amazing, Mom.
Celeste: No way
Dominic: There really are good people in the world.
Celeste: Who do you think sent it?
Me: No idea.
Leilani: The timing is so good
Leilani: So many people need things that we just don't have anymore and now we can get them!!
Jameson: Okay, this is nice and all, but I still need new tires

---

I pull the van up to the curb and put it in park. It's been a month since I got the scratch-off lottery ticket in the mail. It took some time to figure out how to claim the lottery winnings and donate them to Third Friday without hurting myself financially, but once we got it all worked out, we stocked up on the things people had been asking for. Tonight was the first night we were handing out hotdogs in over a year. We'd also gotten some coats from the clearance rack.

"I hope Sally and Bob come tonight!" Leilani says as she opens the passenger door.

I open the driver's door and step out, my boots crunching the snow below my feet. Even Holden has a little extra pep tonight. I don't have to ask him to get out of the van or put his phone down. We get to work setting up the tables and putting out the coffee urns. Leilani helps Holden arrange the hats, gloves, and scarves while I organize the snacks.

The hotdogs are in their buns, wrapped in foil, and stored in a food warmer. The ketchup, mustard, and liquid creamer are sitting beside the sugar packets.

Celeste and Kellen arrive with the take-away bags they filled with two bottles of water, toothbrush and toothpaste, deodorant, menstrual products for women, and some protein bars.

My heart swells with pride and love for my family as heavy, wet snowflakes fall around us, sticking to our hats and coats before they melt. There's joy in the air tonight.

Sure, a cruise would have been nice, and Jameson will figure out how to get tires on his own because not only does he have a car, but a house to live in and a family who loves him. I truly believe the hotdogs and hot chocolate make the world a better place, at least in my small corner of it.

There are days when it seems there is nothing but bad things left in the world. But on an icy, cold winter night, I experienced the good. I will likely never know who scratched off that winning ticket and decided to be selfless and help us help others.

And that's okay.

"Hi, Sophia," Bob calls out as he walks up. "Looks like you got restocked."

I nod. "We got a nice donation."

Sally steps to the table. "You have hotdogs? And mustard?"

"We do." I smile at her. "Would you like one?"

"I would. Thank you."

I hand a foil-wrapped hotdog to Sally. "How's the new apartment coming along?"

"Yeah," Sally says as she peels back the aluminum foil. "We have an apartment now. Me and Bob."

"Do you like it?"

She nods as she squirts mustard onto her hotdog. "Yeah. It's real nice."

I look at Bob beside her. "How's your furniture situation?"

He shrugs. "It's coming along. We've got a table and chairs. An old couch."

"How about a bed?"

"The couch pulls out."

"Aw, okay, that's good." I pause, careful not to overstep. "I'd love to come see your place."

"Me too," Leilani says as she walks toward us. "I'm super happy for you guys."

"Sure, sure," Bob says. "You wanna stop by tomorrow?"

We make plans for the next day.

On our way to Bob and Sally's, we stop and grab a houseplant as a housewarming gift. Bob and Sally's apartment is a sparse one-bedroom with a galley kitchen. Their table and chairs are in the living room with their pull-out couch. A few blankets are folded on the floor in the corner. The bedroom is bare aside from a dresser with drawers that don't shut all the way. Clothes are piled atop it.

"Do you have some dishes and pans?" I ask.

"We have a little bit." Sally opens a cabinet to show some mismatched dishes. Two plates, two bowls, a few plastic cups. "We get those meals on wheels, so we don't have to cook."

I noticed then there was no microwave.

"They sure don't know how to make the food taste good though," she continues.

"I told you, Sal," Bob says. "They can't season it because people have allergies and high blood pressure."

She waves a hand in the air at him. "Yeah, yeah."

"So, what do you guys need the most?"

"A TV," Sally says without hesitating. "Get tired of hearing his voice all the time."

Leilani laughs.

A few hours later, Lelani and I return with a small smart TV, some kitchen things, hangers, toilet paper, and a gift card for the grocery store within walking distance.

While Leilani helps Bob get the TV connected to the building's Wi-Fi, Sally and I put away the kitchen purchases. She pauses when she pulls out a black plastic pasta fork.

"What the heck kind of spoon is this?" she asks.

"It's for pasta."

She holds it at eye level. "How does it work?"

"You use it when you're cooking the noodles, so they don't stick together."

"Hmph." She turns the utensil in her hand. "That's genius."

We finish putting the things away. Sally secures all the plastic bags from the store below the kitchen sink. "You never know when you might need them," she tells me.

Leilani and Bob are exploring the live TV option on the new TV. "And we don't have to pay for this?" Bob asks.

I shake my head. "No, the live TV is free. And there are some movie apps that you can add that don't cost anything. Some of the movies or shows on the apps might have fees, but they'll have plenty of free things, too."

"There's more channels on here than there are on cable TV."

"Leilani, help Bob find some of the apps I'm talking about."

Bob looks over at me. "Thank you, Sophia. This is too kind."

I smile. "I'm just the messenger. This is someone else's doing."

"Well, you're doing a mighty fine job."

Sally sits on the couch. "Does it have a remote?"

Leilani sits beside her. "It does."

"Never had a TV with a remote before," Sally tells us. "My daddy used to make us kids get up and change the channel. We were the remote."

"We had a remote control TV before," Bob reminds Sally. "Plenty of them."

Sally stares at him for a moment, a faraway look in her eyes. "Kids will be home soon."

Bob doesn't answer her. He looks back at the TV as my daughter starts showing them the different shows and movies on a free app she downloaded.

I look out the window of Bob and Sally's seventh-floor apartment at the gray winter sky and notice flurries sifting through the air. "It's snowing again."

"It's snowed a lot this year." Leilani gets up and looks out the window as she hands the remote control to Bob. "More than I remember it snowing when I was a kid."

"You're still a kid," he tells her with a laugh.

"You know what I mean," she says with a smile.

"Every snowflake is different." Sally rises from the couch and joins us at the window. "No two are alike. Kinda like people. Everyone is different but we're all beautiful in our own way." She looks at me. "You know?"

I smile at her. "I do know."

"Winter is cold, but it sure is pretty to look at." Her eyes shift back outside. "Sure am glad we're not out there anymore. But lots of people are. Lots of people would be happy to sleep on the floor in that bedroom we're not using, but they say we can't have people over more than two nights. Just doesn't make sense to make people stay outside in all this snow when we have a perfectly good floor in there with heat. And it's dry." She shakes her head. "I'm sure thankful for the good people in this world, though. Maybe someday we can do nice things for people, too. What do you think, Bob?"

"Like what?"

"Like give people coffee and hotdogs and buy them TVs and fancy spoons."

"If you guys want to help us out, you can," I tell them. "Just meet us on our Fridays and we'll find things for you to do."

Bob nods. "It's the least we can do."

My head falls to the side as I pull my brows together. "No, no. You don't have to. Only if you want to."

"It's a good idea," Bob says. "But some days . . ." He glances back at Sally.

I nod, knowing some days Sally isn't at her best. "You know where to find us."

Leilani and I leave a short while later, the winter air a frigid blast to our faces as we step outside from the overheated apartment building. As we wait a few minutes for the van to warm up, Leilani lets out a sigh.

"What?" I ask.

She shrugs. "Honestly, I was really bummed that we couldn't just keep that money for ourselves. But seeing how excited they were about that hundred-dollar TV made it so worth it. And hearing Sally talk about how people would be happy to sleep on the bedroom floor . . ." Her lips pull in between her teeth. "I don't know. Just makes me realize all I have that other people don't. And that makes me feel selfish for wishing I could have a cruise for my birthday when there are people literally sleeping on the streets." Her gaze shifts to me. "It's just not fair."

"You have a big heart," I tell my daughter as we pull away from the curb in front of Bob and Sally's building. "I hope it never shrinks."

She laughs lightly. "Can we stop for hot chocolate?"

About the Author

Sarah Dawson Powell was born and raised in the suburbs of Chicago and currently lives in Central Illinois with her kidlings and too many cats. Her hobbies include doing laundry, washing dishes, petting cats, writing, reading, and talking to kids who have selective hearing. In her spare time, she enjoys working sixty hours a week, sleeping, and drinking lots of coffee. When she grows up, she wants to change the world.

Sarah has a bachelor's degree in sociology from the University of Illinois and has worked in social services since graduating. Her life hasn't always been peachy, but she's made the best of every situation. No one likes to talk about the dark side of life, so she decided to write books that would give people a glimpse inside of this world. She hopes her readers take something away from her stories and loves to interact with them on social media.

Sarah is the author of The Fragile Line Series and two coming-of-age novels, *The Truth About Gracie* and *In the Moonbeams*.

You can find Sarah on:
Instagram @sarah_dawson_powell
Facebook authorsarahdawsonpowell

And visit her website at www.sarahdawsonpowell.com

COWS & KISSES

Cows & Kisses

T. E. Smith

Chapter 1
Maggie

"DAD, CALM DOWN. BEN AND I will handle getting the herd from the north pasture to the south before the storm hits." I refrain from rolling my eyes at my micromanaging father and lift my coffee cup off the breakfast table.

"No, I'll handle it. It's the middle of winter and it's not going to be an easy trip," he barks, then fills his mouth with eggs and chews vigorously.

I glance over at my mom, who shakes her head slightly before standing and walking to the kitchen with the empty bacon plate.

The man is downright insufferable when it comes to running this ranch, but he had a heart attack last month and the doctor still has not cleared him. Though, that hasn't stopped the old man from trying. Normally, I would back down and respect his authority, but that isn't an option when it means risking his health.

"You're right, it won't be easy, and that is why Ben is coming, too. The doctor didn't clear you to ride yet. So, I'll handle this just like I've been handling everything else on this ranch." I set my jaw and meet his gaze, leaving no room for argument. His mouth is pressed into a firm and annoyed line, but so is mine. I will argue this with him all day if I have to, but we both know that will do us no good with the storm approaching.

Mom glides back into the room with some fresh fruits and sets them down next to Dad. "See, dear, Ben is going, too. They can handle this. Then this afternoon you and I can take the truck with fresh hay out to the south pasture to help." She knows just how to give him exactly what he needs yet keep him from doing too much. I guess you learn a thing or two when you have been married for twenty-seven years.

Ben is a huge reason I have managed the ranch so well over the past month. His family owns the neighboring ranch, so we grew up together. Most of our childhood was spent either at their place or ours, and we always found some sort of mischief to get into. And it was usually always Ben's idea.

After our ranch hand quit, Dad and I were struggling to handle all the ranch duties ourselves, even pre-heart attack. Ben was more than happy to take a job with us. He has three older brothers managing his family's ranch, so he was going to be looking for a ranch hand job soon anyway. I don't like to think about it, but I'm honestly not sure how I would have managed this ranch without him after Dad went down.

My dad slams his silverware down in frustration. "When did I die, and this ranch become both of yours to manage?"

"Dad, I meant no disrespect." I relax my features to try and bring peace to his fury. "I'm only trying to take care of you. You'll be back to running everything in no time. Just for now, please let me handle moving the cattle," I plead, praying he will concede.

He eyes me, and I can see the war in his features.

"Fine. Leave after breakfast," he grumbles. "What the hell do doctors know anyway?" He lifts his coffee, taking a large swallow.

I chuckle under my breath. "Sure thing. We'll be back before you know it."

"And tell Ben that I expect him to be the perfect gentleman."

"He always is, Dad, you know that." I smirk at him, always the overprotective father.

The rest of breakfast was pleasant, and my mother gave him a chore list he was actually allowed to do in our absence, which relaxed him a bit more.

"Some of your thermal wear is still in your old room if you need a bit more," my mom offers as I place the dishes in the sink.

I moved out last year, only to the guest cottage, though. I am twenty-three and still living on the family property, rent free, and the only job I have is running the ranch with Dad. So much for me being a strong independent woman, right? But honestly, I wouldn't have it any other way. This ranch will be mine to look after someday and it's the only job I've ever seen myself doing. This is where I want to be.

"Thanks, Mom, but I should be set." I smile at her, moving toward the door to put on my boots.

"Okay, well, take a camp pack just in case, and be safe." She follows me and gives me a hug.

"Will do. I love you, Mom."

With that, she releases me, and I head out the door toward the barn.

Excitement fills me, and I add a spring to my step. I haven't had a full day of moving cattle in months because usually Dad handles it. I love riding the pastures with my gelding, Blaze, and I get to go with Ben, so it is sure to be an adventure.

Back when we were about fourteen, he had the bright idea to try and ride one of our heifers when Dad was in town for the day. I did not partake in that, but I did help pick him up out of the mud when he was done, because, as I'd predicted, he was not the prodigy bull rider he'd imagined himself to be.

With it being just the two of us today, I have no doubt he'll do something ridiculous. He likes to let his troublemaking side off the leash when Dad is not around, and I would be lying if I said I wasn't excited to be his partner in crime.

Chapter 2
Ben

WE'LL SEE IF SHE ACTUALLY manages to convince Jeff to let us move the cattle without him. The man is as stubborn as they come, but he has always had a soft spot for Maggie.

I mean, who wouldn't have a soft spot for that sweet and sassy little thing? She's always full of joy, but somehow manages to have the attitude of a mule. I am thankful that she has never ventured to the bar with me, because she would throw down with the biggest person there, like she isn't a five-foot blonde toothpick.

Pulling my truck up to the barn, I climb out, coffee in hand. It's about to be a cold, snowy day with a light dusting of snowflakes falling already. It's not ideal weather to ride in, but if we don't move the cows, they'll be out of hay, and we won't be able to get to them with more. Plus, the south pasture has more shelter for them to brave the storm under.

Jeff's barn is small, with only four horse stalls and a tiny office that doubles as a tack room, but it's always done the job. I lead Maggie's horse, Blaze, from his stall. He is a chestnut-colored gelding with white socks on his legs and a fiery disposition. He suits Maggie well; they share the same attitude.

After fastening him to the tie ring on the wall, I pull out my mare,

Comet, next. She has been my smooth and steady ride for the past four years, but I got lucky. I bought her simply because of how beautiful she was at an auction. She is a dappled gray quarter horse, and I had to have her. I figured if she was a bad ride, she would make a beautiful broodmare, but thankfully, she rides like a dream.

Once Comet is settled next to Blaze, I get them ready for the day ahead. I really hope it's just Maggie and me. Don't get me wrong, Jeff is a great boss, but Maggie has become the person I look forward to seeing the most, and she doesn't even know it.

"Morning, Cowboy!" She swoops in the door, with snowflakes on her eyelashes making her blue eyes sparkle.

"Good morning." I smile at her as she walks over to Blaze and pets his neck. She looks incredible in her tight jeans and Carhart coat, with her blond hair flowing down her back. I can't help but stare at her.

"Thanks for getting a jump on saddling Blaze. It's just going to be the two of us today, so we need to get going or we won't be back until late." She smiles at me and my chest swells with excitement that Jeff won't be joining us.

"Of course. Comet is almost ready and then we can hit the trail," I assure her as she disappears into the office.

I should have taken a chance and asked her out already, but we're really good as friends, and I don't want to risk that. Or make things awkward between me and Jeff.

But she's all I think about.

On my way to work, I'm excited to see her.

At work, I find excuses to be with her.

After work, I dream about her.

I have been pining after this woman since high school, and I envy the man who wins her heart.

She comes out of the tack room with a camp pack and fastens it to the back of her saddle.

"Why the camp pack? It's only a day's ride."

"I know. I just told Mom I would bring one to be safe."

The camp packs don't hold much—a small tent, a fire starter, a blanket, instant coffee, a small kettle, and three dehydrated meals—but it's better than nothing.

"Oh, you want me to grab one, too?" I ask as I finish the last of my preparations.

"No, we're not going to need them. Mom is just being overprotective, as usual." She chuckles and rolls her eyes at the statement. "You ready?"

"Yep, let's head out." I untie Comet as she leads Blaze from the barn.

Today will be fun. The snow is falling, the horses are calm, the Montana Mountains are a great view, and I get to spend the day with my best friend.

Chapter 3
Maggie

THE TRAIL TO THE NORTH pasture is my favorite. The mountains up ahead with the trees on either side always makes for a breathtaking ride, but with the light snow flurries, it's making it feel absolutely magical.

The horses are handling the snow well, so we're making decent time. As long as the cows move easily, we should be back to the house well before nightfall.

Per usual, Ben and I have joked and laughed throughout the trip so far, and I'm well aware that a smile has been plastered on my face all morning. He is just a joy to be around and a total marshmallow, but you wouldn't know it by looking at him. The man is a truck! Easily six-five with broad shoulders, shaggy black hair that is always covered by his well-worn cowboy hat, and biceps that strain his T-shirts. How this man has not been locked down yet by one of the girls in town, I'll never know.

"Maggie!" Ben calls from behind me. Turning in my saddle to look at him, I catch him pulling some snow off a low-hanging branch.

"Don't do it, Cowboy." I smile with anticipation, because I know it's said in vain.

"Oh, I'm going to do it." He wickedly grins as he forms the snow into a ball in his hand.

"No—"

But before I can get out the rest, I am nailed in the back with a cold, hard snowball.

I squeal and laugh at the impact as snow flies around me.

"This is war now!" I declare as I spur Blaze forward to get to the next branch. He takes off and we make it to the branch well before Ben. I form a nice tight snowball and wait for him to get close enough.

When Ben is within a good range, I don't hesitate as I hit him squarely in the chest. "Haha! Gotcha!" I proudly tease.

"That's the only shot you get, so you better move it." He teases back.

We both take off for the next branch, but Comet has always been faster than Blaze. Ben beats me to the branch, and in record time, he forms the snowball and flings it at me.

With a *thump*, it smacks Blaze in the shoulder instead of me. He whinnies loud, rearing high off his front legs, and shoots forward. He whinnies again, and I focus on keeping my seat. This isn't my first rodeo with him, and after growing up on a ranch, it's like my mind and body know what to do, but my stomach is in my throat all the same.

"Whoa boy . . . Easy . . ." I try to soothe him, but he rears again. The snow in my saddle has my butt sliding, and I lose the balance I was desperately hanging on to.

I hit the ground on my side with a painful *thwump*. Pain shoots through my hip.

Goodness, that hurt.

"MAGGIE!" Ben bellows, and within seconds he is sliding onto the ground next to me.

"Are you hurt?" His eyes frantically search mine and he starts feeling my limbs, checking me over with such a tender touch, it makes butterflies erupt in my belly.

"No, I think I'm good," I say as I try to catch my breath a little and shift to sit up. Blaze thankfully didn't bolt after his episode and is standing next to us, while Comet stands right next to him, where Ben left her.

It always amazes me how smart and loving horses are. Blaze should have taken off, but with me no longer in the saddle, I became the priority.

"Are you sure?" His voice is downright panicked as he looks me over.

"Ben, calm down. I have had worse falls than this. Nothing that a heating pad won't cure later."

He releases a sigh of relief and lifts me to his lap, wrapping me in his strong arms.

"I am so sorry, Maggie. When I saw you fall, I worried Blaze was going to land on you if he reared up again." He holds me for a long moment before he whispers, "I've got you, Darlin'. You're safe now."

I have never allowed myself to look at Ben as anything more than a friend, but this is different. Here and now, as I listen to the thump of his heartbeat and feel the warmth and strength of his arms, my heart has never felt so full. I don't want this moment to end.

Chapter 4
Ben

MAGGIE WAS SORE AS I helped her back up onto Blaze; she was stiff as a board and winced when she sat down. There is no doubt in my mind that she will have a nasty bruise in an hour or two. I am such an idiot. My horsing around almost got her seriously hurt. Part of me wishes there had been more snow already; the journey would have been harder, but it would have cushioned her fall. Guilt has been rolling in my stomach ever since, despite Maggie's assurance that she is okay and her "no need for apology" responses.

"Look, there's the herd!" she cheers.

The cows are at the most northern part of the pasture all huddled together.

"Alright, let's get to work," I grumble as I walk Comet forward.

"Seriously, Ben!" she snaps behind me. I turn in my seat to look at her scowling face.

Good, she should be mad at me.

"You need to get over yourself. I am not working the rest of the day with you as a grumpy jerk because of an accident."

"It wasn't an accident!" I bark at her.

She pulls Blaze to a stop, raising her eyebrows at me, knowing well enough it was.

"Oh, so you *meant* to hit Blaze instead of me?"

"You know I didn't—"

"Then it was an accident, Ben. So, forgive yourself and get over it."

And that's that. Conversation over. She takes off with Blaze toward the herd.

I drop my head and shake it before following behind her. I should've known she would win this one, because she wins everything. I would give that girl the moon if she asked it of me. I have never even taken her on a single date, but we don't need to date for me to know that girl holds my heart. She has been there for me in every good time and bad. When I do something stupid, she is always there to help me up and tell me I'm an idiot. When I am overwhelmed, she is the first to help me carry the load. And when I am at the top of my game, she is always in the background cheering me on. She has been my ride or die since the third grade.

We became friends because Patrick Marlow was picking on me at recess for having hand-me-down clothes with holes in them from my brothers. Maggie stepped in like the whirlwind she is, demanding that he leave me be. When Patrick told her, "Beat it, this is boys' business," she decked him in the nose and made the boy bleed like a stuck pig. That evening, I went to her house to thank her for standing up for me, and the rest was history.

Maggie is currently pushing the cows from behind, while I keep the herd together on the sides, but we're moving slower than we should be. The snow is deeper in the pasture with the lack of tree coverage.

It's evening now, and we are only three quarters of the way to the south pasture. We only have maybe an hour left before the temperature starts to drop and we lose daylight.

Worry swirls in my gut, because there is no way we are making it back to the ranch tonight and it tends to get *cold* out here.

"Maggie, I think we better stop and make camp."

"No, let's keep pushing." She's determined as she spurs Blaze forward.

"Come on, cows! Move it!" she scolds them.

"If we don't stop now, we won't be able to make a fire before nightfall, and there is no way we are making it back to the ranch tonight. Plus, there's some hay still accessible beneath the snow on the round bale over there, so the cows won't wander." I've argued with Jeff many times on not needing hay in four different spots in the pasture, and right now I'm so thankful he never listened to me.

She lets out a sigh and her shoulders slack. "Fine. I'll back off, ride up, and stop the herd."

Thank you, Lord above, that she conceded. There are times she is more stubborn than her dad, and that's saying something.

After stopping the cows, they venture to the hay and Maggie dismounts. "You go get the firewood and I'll set up the tent." She leads Blaze to a nearby tree.

Anticipation and nervous energy fill me at the realization that we only have one camp pack.

Chapter 5
Maggie

THE WARM FIRE CRACKLES IN front of us as we eat dinner. Ben is a born and raised country man; he also managed to find us a log to sit on.

The blanket from the pack covers us both, but the chill of the evening is still intense. Winter camping in the Montana wilderness is definitely something to be avoided.

The coffee was put over the fire a while ago, and I cannot wait for the warmth to fill me as a small shiver runs through my body.

"You cold?" Ben looks at me with concern in his eyes.

"You're not?" I tease with a chuckle.

"Come here." He pulls me closer to him and wraps his strong arms around me.

Sparks fly over my skin at his touch, and I shiver again for a whole other reason.

"I'll help keep you warm until the coffee is ready." He rubs his hand up and down my arms, warming me, and I am tempted to say I never want that coffee to be ready.

"Thank you," I speak softly as I look up to meet his warm gaze.

"I will always take care of you, Darlin'."

Warmth fills my chest at his words, and all I want is to kiss the man who has always been there for me. The man who can make me laugh when no one else can, the one who has been there as a shoulder for me to cry on, the one who has always been there to cheer me on . . . my best friend.

When we were sixteen, my first boyfriend, Carter, broke up with me. Ben was right there on the couch with me that evening with a tub of ice cream, offering to let all the air out of his tires at school the next day so he would have to get a ride.

When I tried running for class president my senior year, Ben was low-key bribing everyone with promises of a party at his place if I won—with beer, of course. His heart was in the right place, always my personal cheerleader, even if his methods were not the best.

When I decided to move into the guest house, he was there to lend all the muscle I needed and help with the small tedious jobs like painting.

Then this summer, we went to our favorite swimming and fishing spot at Gosling Lake after a long day of moving hay. The water was so cold on my toes that I refused to go in, but Ben threw me over his shoulder, saying, "Oh no, you're not getting out of this one!"

I squealed and thrashed against his hold, but he tossed me in off the dock. I was horrified, but he quickly cannonballed in next to me. The evening was filled with fun, laughter, and water fights. When we were done, I realized I'd left my towel at home, and he didn't hesitate to give me his, to make sure I was taken care of. He had the same look in his eyes then that he does now. I just never recognized it for what it was before this moment.

He clears his throat and pulls his eyes away to look out at the cows, but I am a bold woman. I grab his chin and pull his gaze back to mine.

"Maybe it's the snow or the fire but . . ." I pause as my heart leaps to my throat. "I would like you to kiss me, Cowboy."

His eyes light up and a smirk forms on his face. He tips my chin up and moves so his lips are brushing mine. "I have wanted to kiss you forever, Maggie Parker."

He kisses me softly, pouring every ounce of love for me into it. I have kissed a few men in my life, but none have ever kissed me back like this. My heart feels fit to burst out of my chest as I pull him deeper to me, savoring his pillow-soft lips, his sweet taste, and the feel of his hands on me, until the whistle of the kettle breaks us apart.

He moves quickly, pulling it from the fire, then brings me back to him and rests his forehead against mine. "That was incredible, Darlin', and now I am never going to let you go."

The snowflakes twinkle around us in the glow of the firelight, with the stars shining above us. The horses' hooves crunch snow, and the cows moo in the distance as a light breeze passes through. There is something so simple and perfect to this evening. I press myself closer to him as I whisper, "I never want you to let me go, Cowboy."

Chapter 6
Ben

THE REALITY OF HAVING MAGGIE in my arms is better than I could have ever dreamed, and I hate that I didn't pursue her sooner. She is true perfection with her smile, attitude, kind heart, and a gorgeous body.

The rest of the evening consisted of us often kissing and cuddling in the small tent. It was dual purpose: we both were able to stay warm, and I got to hold her close all night long. I have been in love with the rancher's daughter for far too long to waste any time now.

We have to get back to the ranch today, because we're out of food and the storm will be upon us soon. So, we get up and moving at the first sign of light.

"You get enough coffee, Darlin'?" I ask before dumping what little is left and putting out the fire.

"Yeah, all set!" she yells from next to Blaze, where she is tying down her saddle.

I carry over the camp pack, and throw it up onto her horse, to start securing it.

"How's your hip?" I ask, touching it gently and wanting nothing more than to check it myself.

"Stiff, but I'm fine." She gives me a smile that warms every inch of me.

"You will see the doctor when we get back." Accidents happen from time to time, and I have had my fair share of falls. This is different, though. She fell because of me, didn't have access to any self-care items, and at the very least a doctor can make sure nothing has a hairline fracture.

"Ever the caretaker, Cowboy," she teases and rolls her eyes as she wraps her arms around me.

"I'm serious, Maggie," I scold her, but she just smiles.

"Shut up and kiss me before we hit the trail."

I hold her gaze, but in the end I relent. I kiss her deep and hard, savoring every second of her sweetness so it will last me until I can kiss her again. Part of me still cannot believe I get to do this now.

After we part, I walk with her to Blaze's side and give her a leg up into her saddle. A cool wind whips through, and a slight uneasiness hits me. The clouds are darkening, and this storm could be on us before we even get back.

Chapter 7
Maggie

AFTER THE COLD NIGHT, THE cows seem much more eager to move now that the wind is picking up. The clouds are growing dark, and I can tell Ben is slightly worried. He's checking the sky way more frequently than he did yesterday.

Ben and I are working the same formation as yesterday, except now the cows are moving faster, and he keeps making teasing jabs about me falling behind. I'm not, but it doesn't stop him from picking on me. Every teasing remark falls a little flat, so I can tell he's just masking the stress we both feel with his humor. That storm is too close for comfort, and I don't think he wants me to see how concerned he actually is.

It's close to lunch time when we finally make it to the south pasture. The cows huddle around the fresh hay that my parents had successfully placed yesterday, as planned, and finally, our work is done.

"The storm is coming in." I nod toward the clouds behind us. The snow started picking up about an hour ago. We need to get back to the barn before we get stuck out here.

"Yeah, it will probably be on us in an hour or so. Race you back into the barn?" Ben smiles at me with that same wicked glint that he always has when he's up to something.

"Want to make it interesting?" I shrug my shoulders, trying to be nonchalant.

"With you, always." His voice is honeyed with temptation.

"Loser tells Dad we're together."

"You're on, Darlin'."

Turning Blaze, I spur him forward and we take off through the field as fast as the snow will allow. Comet has always been faster, but I play dirty as I direct Blaze to keep them from passing.

"Play fair!" Ben yells from behind me.

"Not a chance!" I toss over my shoulder as the barn comes into view.

Pushing Blaze to go faster, Comet makes it around us. *Good thing I have the trump card...*

Comet and Ben make it just outside the barn first and Ben looks like he just won All-Around Rider at the rodeo or something.

I pull Blaze to a stop and leap off him. "You said *into* the barn!" I yell as I run Blaze to the barn.

"You cheat!" he shouts.

"Not cheating, just winning." I laugh and slide into the barn first.

I laugh again as he comes in the barn wearing a huge smile to match my own. He approaches me and places his hands on my hips.

"I guess you win, Darlin'."

"I sure do." I reach up, grabbing his hat and placing it on my head.

"Maggie." His voice turns deep and husky. "You're wearing my hat."

"Sure am. Now kiss me, Cowboy, because I have waited too long for you to do it."

He kisses me passionately, and warmth blooms in my chest as fire erupts between us. I'm not sure what the future holds, but I do know one thing.

"I think I've always loved you, Cowboy."

"I know I've always loved you, Darlin'."

The moment is interrupted when someone clears their throat from the door of the barn. Ben whirls around, and we grasp each other's hands—perhaps partly in solidarity and perhaps partly in fear—at the sight of my dad leaning against the door frame with his arms crossed.

"So," he starts, and his voice sounds deeper, raspier, the same way it gets when he is trying not to yell, "not only did you barely make it back before the storm, but now I walk in on you two clowns kissing."

His face is flat as he eyes us. A moment of silence stretches on, and it feels like an eternity as I wait for his response. He had warned me to tell Ben to be the perfect gentleman, so he may actually be upset. Crap! He won't fire him, will he?

Slowly, a smirk forms on his face. "Well, I guess I should thank the cows for moving slow, because I was beginning to think you two were never going to get together."

He chuckles and shakes his head as he leaves the barn once more.

What? He knew? I guess Dad is still the wisest man I know.

Ben leans over and places a soft kiss on my forehead. "Well, I guess I don't have to tell your dad we're together now," he teases.

I smack him on the chest, and he laughs like the troublemaking cowboy he is. But the thing is . . . he is now *my* troublemaking cowboy, and I wouldn't change him for anything.

About the Author

J.E. Smith is a romance enthusiast who loves to write sassy heroines and book boyfriends that you'll wish were real. She loves to write into the late hours of the night or at a local coffee shop with something sweet nearby. She is a West Michigan native, residing in a small town outside of Grand Rapids, where she enjoys the country life with her amazing husband, four wild children, two dogs, and a cat. When she is not writing or lost in a new book, she enjoys exploring the outdoors with her family, traveling, and going on silly adventures.

You can find J.E. Smith on:
Instagram @author_j.e.smith
Facebook AuthorJ.E.Smith
TikTok @j.e.smith.author

And visit her website at www.bio.site/JEsmith

SUNBEAM

Sunbeam

Guihan Larsen

BEFORE YOU LEFT FOR VIETNAM, I proffered up a wax paper Archie's comic strip tucked inside my bubblegum wrapper that smelled like pink dust.

"Is it funny?" you said.

"Yeah."

"Only want it if it's funny."

In the kitchen, you jimmied the back door open with a screwdriver. With the heel of your palm, you whacked the top and slid the flathead down along the seam, chipping away the early November's ice. Your head bent down, your face set in a practiced grimace, as you banked rafts of ice nestled on the rusted shovel out and away from the house. I felt the weight of each hunk of whiteness as it thudded to the side. Your hands turned red and rash while you slapped them against your pants popcorned in snow.

Ma warned over the electric hum of her mixer, "You need your gloves."

"Nah."

The sound stopped, as if it had gone for a distant walk only to tread softly backward. The scent of chocolate so strong I wanted to bite the air.

Once cleared, you shoved the screen door open onto a backyard hidden beneath a sea of snow.

Finished, you stomped in. Both of you, face to face. Ma wiped her hands down along the front of her housecoat, patterned with red-nosed reindeer and cigarette burns. Then, a pocket of silence before Ma's chin started to quiver, before she grabbed you by the coat collar and sobbed.

"I don't know why you insisted on going out this way. The front door is perfectly clear." Ma's voice was low and muffled.

"Just easier. I shoulda fixed it before. Nothing like waiting to the last minute, huh?"

"Leave tomorrow?"

"Nah. Better now."

A sweat of ice outlined your spit-black shoes as you leaned over the counter to wolf down a brownie.

"Aww, too bad these aren't any good. Don't eat 'em," you said to me.

I sucked in cold lake air as you swung your green duffle up and over.

The month before you went off to war, you brought home Shoot-the-Moon. A present for us. The game involved the balance of a silver ball bearing along an inclined pair of steel rods fixed at one end, maneuvering the free ends together and apart, and then the careful descent onto the indentations on the wood base below. I liked the craters the ball dropped into, each named after a planet: Mercury, Earth, Mars, Jupiter, Saturn, and the closest, Pluto, gave the highest score. As the days leading up to your departure began to latch together, your movements turned faraway and jittery. You didn't have the steady hand needed for the game but blamed it on not having the patience, and so, passed it along for me to play.

After you were gone, I picked up strands of tinsel from the floor, straggled leftovers from the party in the basement thrown for you and your friends. Through the hazy orange light and guitar music ringed with chimes, girls had danced all by themselves to "Get Together." Their eyes closed as if in a trance. Their pixie hairdos made them look like elves from one of my books.

I gathered the glittering squiggles and made a row of silver soldiers along the tabletop, tasked as custodians of the butter dish. Ma sat next to me and twirled the ash of her cigarette along the edge of a chipped teacup until it formed a point. We stayed side by side until her cigarette's red glow was the only light apart from the dim twinkle circling the tree.

After a few weeks, a letter came. Left tented on top of the TV, traced with orphaned fingertips, the stationery browned around its edges. You wrote stories of rats as big as cats and a game of throwing warm, woolen socks onto the bunks of sleeping soldiers designed to make them think creatures were jumping on them. The socks were sent from Ma, who hadn't realized the temperature where you were stationed was in the seventies. You described the new surroundings, how the fridge at the base was stocked with only beer and Royal Crown Cola, and being rocketed or mortared every day, and sometimes twice! I wrote a letter back about how I stayed in the kitchen while the nightly news was on so I wouldn't hear the gunfire.

In another letter, you wrote: *We were riding in a copter, and, guess what? There was snow in the mountains. Somehow, in the north, the fog lifted, and down below in this place called Sapa, snow was on the terraced rice fields. It looked like a layer cake. I swear, we all cheered when we saw the sight. The socks Ma sent finally had another purpose.*

You missed the big snowflakes back home, the way the snow clouds turned everything quiet and numb, and how our block smelled like pastrami and burning wood in the winter. The smell of flurries, even when the snow turned chunky and gray. You missed the slosh. The *Trib* rolled up and tucked under your coat and how the sweet smell of paper and ink became prominent in the wintertime.

Then, you sent a necklace—a ladybug, bright red with big black dots whose wings opened to reveal a watch inside. I timed my walk from the school bus to home. My mittens made it impossible to open the buttons of my coat, so I sucked on the ends and let the ice melt, pretending the wool was soaked in orange sherbet before my free hand was able to grab the ladybug.

Passing by houses still fancied up with decorations, the wind carried scents of cinnamon from wood piles and chestnuts from chimneys. Boys flew out the doors with sleds and scarves to their noses. Their little sisters marched after them. The snow fell first in bits and pieces, fluffy white cotton tips blown in a swirl caught around my coat collar and melted down my neck. I sat on a pile of splits until the row of houses on our block came alive with jewelry lights. Mothers moved in and out of view, and fathers rumbled onto graveled driveways, gray exhaust flooded from the back of their cars until engines were turned off. I knew Dad wouldn't be coming back to us, and by then his face was in a slow dissolve. But, somehow, I thought maybe if I stayed still and hoped hard enough, time would reverse.

I sat for too long. The ladybug wings were left open, so the snow had mixed in and froze the watch to where it no longer worked. I huffed hot air on the dial in an attempt to revive the inner workings with warmth, but the ticking had stopped.

I didn't tell Ma or write to you about the watch. Instead, I slid the bug up and down the length of its chain while I assisted Ma at her new ritual.

Once a month, her auburn hair peeked out underneath a paisley kerchief as she brought out her Sunbeam Mixmaster to make brownies. Silence aside from the whir of beaters swirling through batter. Her lips pursed as she scraped the tip of a rubber spatula along the inner rim of the bowl. Then, her fingers paddled against the outside of the cool silver while her hand palmed the bowl 'round and 'round the turntable spinner. I licked the whisk until the batter formed a velvet mustache on my upper lip.

"Why are they called brownies?"

"After the áes sídhe who come out at night to help with the kitchen chores. It might be your nanna's ghost. She worked as a scullery maid when she came over to this country."

Ma poured the mix into a dusted pan, placed it on the rack, and closed the oven door in a whisper.

"The áes sídhe get mad if you leave them bread, and so, you have to make something sweet and portable and more satisfying than a cookie to take on their journey."

The scent of chocolate wafted from the oven and made me sleepy. I rested my forehead on my arms and had dreams of soft snow and cottontail rabbits capped with goldfinch tams leaping over our house.

Once cooled, placed in a tin, and wrapped up in a paper bag from Jewel Grocery, Ma posted the brownies off to you. I sat on the stool at our Formica kitchen table and bit into a melty chocolate square and imagined them being flown over your base in Biên Hòa, dropping down, down, down.

It was wintertime when I came back to our house and rummaged through stuff in the attic in my halfhearted attempt to clean it out. From the window, the houses down below looked like a row of kneeling brides. A Polaroid of you, Ma, Dad, and me, taken a few years before he split and you left for Nam. A scrawl in her handwriting on the back, *Mitch '65*. Ma with her checkered apron cinched around the waist and a bit of a smile. In her blue dress, she is seated on the kitchen chair with a look of exhaustion. Dad, on a chair next to her, in a white T-shirt, spent and unshaven, with flecks of white paint in his hair. He holds me on his lap almost as an afterthought. Behind Ma, your hand rests on her shoulder. You're in a white button-down shirt and black pants. You look off to the side, eyes cast down, mouth slightly open, unsmiling.

Your clothes hang loose against your thin body.

Frozen air rushes in from the window, a slivered opening spiders the pane. I tugged at my cardigan to pull around my growing belly. Unable to stop rummaging, I sift through boxes filled with papers in various stages of moth and rust until I come across Ma's old cookbook and find the recipe smudged and stained.

Brownies

- 1 cup sugar
- ¼ cup melted butter
- 1 egg, unbeaten
- 2 squares Baker's chocolate, melted
- ¾ teaspoon vanilla
- ½ cup flour
- ½ cup walnut meats, cut in pieces

Mix ingredients in order given. Line a seven-inch square pain in paraffine paper. Spread mixture evenly in pan and bake in a slow oven. As soon as taken from oven turn pan, remove paper, and cut cake in strips, using a sharp knife. If these directions are not followed paper will cling to cake, and it will be impossible to cut it in shapely pieces.

My heartbeat steadied with the creak of the wood floors beneath my socked feet. "No nuts, more chocolate," I said, out loud. The word *paraffine*—like a window wreathed with snowflakes, delicate and temporary. Directions warn me about the danger of clinging, otherwise, there won't be a shape.

Later at night, I jimmy the back door open with the flathead I found in the junk drawer. With a push, the door opens against a berm of snow, and I am in a quarry of alabaster that shimmers under the moon. I take the silver ball bearing from our game and hold it up to the moonlight.

"Like this?" I ask you. *Yeah.* I hear your voice. I let the ball roll down my palm, dropped loose, it lands in the snow.

I've read somewhere mothers in Vietnam experience dreams, in which the spirit of their boy speaks to them. There are unknown martyrs' graves in Vietnam containing remains. Hoping to track down where their dead sons are located, in order to give them a proper burial so that their souls may finally rest in peace, they consulted geomancers. The geomancer is able to locate for them which of the dozens upon dozens of unknown martyr's graves contain the remains of their son. Hopeful mothers kneel on straw mats until a geomancer sketches out color-coded maps of green whorls on torn-off lengths of poster paper indicating a possible location. Then a handful of soil is tossed to the ground and through the interpretation of lines and textures brought forth from the earth, the circulating soul is located.

There are eighty-two such graveyards in Vietnam. And slowly, recently, the spirits of the lost are finally being located—after a decades-long hiatus in which millions of screaming souls circulated unendingly through the ether without a firm place to land.

The only thing I have carried with me throughout my life is the Sunbeam mixing bowl. I wait until winter, and it's then my kitchen fills with the scent of chocolate and clouds of vanilla, and this is when I think of you and Ma at the kitchen door on that winter morning, and of the impossible notion of that day.

Brownie recipe appears in: Farmer, Fannie Merritt; *Boston Cooking School* (Boston, Mass.) Little, Brown, and Company, Boston, [c1918].

About the Author

Guihan Larsen is a writer from Chicago. Her fiction and flash fiction stories have appeared in numerous anthologies and literary journals. Her work has been featured in *Querencia Press*, *Autumn 2024 Anthology*, and *OFIC Magazine, Issue #10*, among other publications. She has received support from the Elizabeth George Foundation and the Ucross Foundation. Guihan holds an MFA from Columbia University and is currently at work on a novel. She lives in New York, where she boards dogs who keep her company as she writes.

You can find Guihan Larsen on:
Instagram @guihanlarsen
LinkedIn guihanlarsenwriter

PRAIRIE TALE

Prairie Tale
A Little Girl's Winter Night
Amy Kelly

FAIRY KISSES OF SNOWFLAKES BRUSH her cheeks and rest on her eyelashes, bidding her to wake. Her hand stirs into consciousness.

Was that a wooden handle it grasped?

There is cold beneath her. Her head aches as she surfaces through recent memory. Ice. Black ice at the foot of the well. Its rock walls loom above her like a tombstone in the white-blanketed landscape. Blank like her mind as it searches for meaning and context.

What had she been doing?

A woman moaning in the distance. Her heart and ears ache from the mournful sounds. Was that the wind whipping through the plains, screaming like an evil queen?

Had she wandered barefoot into Lapland and onto the path of the Snow Queen's palace?

No, Mama had told her to pull her boot laces tight on such a night. The memory pokes at her from her fog.

Mama! she realizes.

That was why Mary lay here before the well, overturned bucket in her hand. Spilled water she needed to boil. Mama had sent her out here to fetch it from the well.

Cold, uncertain hands had pulled on frozen ropes, burning with the effort of it, the frost had bitten her with each pull. Water from the dark, damp, earthy depths had emerged. The bucket filled. That's when she had slipped.

Now there is the taste of copper, and iron, and something darker. Is that blood in her mouth?

Slow to get up, her limbs are like heavy stones and her head throbs. The spilled water is now ice on her bonnet and calico dress, the shell buttons frozen shut. The paradoxical burn of cold sets in.

The bucket needs to be filled again. Fumbling with the cord, she brings up the bucket again, hand over hand, the ache of it nearly putting her back on the ground as pain twists its icy grasp around her.

She turns to go back to the house but has been pulled into a vortex of white. She has lost the house somehow. The familiar paths she skipped along on sunny days has been swallowed by a white abyss.

Where am I? she wonders, teeth chattering.

The snowstorm, a dense swarm of white bees humming and covering the landscape, prevents her from finding her path, her way home to Mama. Mary closes her eyes and thinks of Gerta and Kai escaping a winter palace in one of her fairy tales. Details she strains the reach of her memory to grasp, the effort making her dizzy as she walks.

A little way in one direction, only a few spills, her legs shuffling through the molasses pull of the drifts and her fatigue, she walks straight into old Rusty's house. The stoic hound is snug from the storm in the little red house Pa had built him.

Next to this is a timber-framed barn. The cows, Betsy and Babe, softly moo and seem unaware of the storm, unaffected by the shriek of the wind . . . or was that the witch?

Mary considers staying in the barn, in the hay, curled up beside the warm bodies of the animals as their breath rhythmically lulls her to sleep.

With the next scream, though, she knows she has to get back to Mama.

Starting with a run, careful not to spill or fall again, she moves toward the screams and finds herself at the edge of a wood. An owl hoots in the nook of its tree, reminding her of her papa's warning about what could befall a young girl in the forest. Danger lurks in that copse of trees, naked winter branches reaching out like the bony fingers of Baba Yaga, her shivering chicken legs crouched in wait to pluck any little girl foolish enough to approach the wooded edge.

The yard is so big and so covered by the endless falling snow. Her Mama needs her, but where is she? Mary feels her chest tense. Her heart thuds.

Are those hooves? she wonders. *Could Papa be back already? Or is it the sleigh of the Snow Queen? Reindeer pulling, whipped in cruelty, their mouths foaming from the effort of it?*

Her thoughts and uncertainty begin to swirl in her mind like the white whorls of snow whipped in front of her. Panic grips her. Run and fight the evil queen or lose herself to the white abyss.

This is the work of a troll king, Mary thinks. He fiendishly arranged so many shards of mirror that all that was reflected was white.

White.

Stark white.

Infinite white.

No up. No down. Just empty.

A void.

Moving risks getting more lost and staying still means certain death. Tears prick her eyes, and she puts the bucket down to wipe them, careful to lean the handle against her shins so she can find it by feel in the storm, though she can no longer feel her fingers or toes. She wishes she was a character in one of her books; they always know what to do. She sobs, immobilized. Surely the Snow Queen will win this time. Snowflake guards will approach at any moment, their cold blue spears of ice poised to pierce her heart. Slumping down beside her bucket, she resigns to her imminent execution. In her last moment, she remembers what Ma and Pa would want her to do.

"Our father, who art in heaven . . ." She closes her eyes, the words emerging from the far reaches of her mind. She pulls them from memories of Ma and Pa sitting by the fire. Ma darning socks and Pa oiling his boots, while she lay on her quilt reading. Warm, sweet memories flood her as she prays. *This was what it felt like to be Sleeping Beauty*, she thinks, lulled into a heavy slumber forever. She opens her eyes for one last look at the world she knew before leaving it.

The snow seems to funnel suddenly, and at the end, the gentle glow of the window. Mary breathes in and tucks her brown hair under her bonnet.

Could that be Mama sitting by the fireplace, rocking her way through her moans? She had to find out. Can she escape the Snow Queen's grasp? Mary pulls her heavy limbs up and picks up the bucket.

Go toward the faint glowing light.

Each step grows her determination. Any moment, the truth will reveal itself. More white and death, or the house and she will be saved.

There it is.

There is the glow from the window of the one-room log house Papa had built last summer with the neighbor. Warmth pours through her heart and back upon realizing she has found it. She will be inside with Mama at any moment.

Pushing up the wooden latch, fumbling frozen fingers, she nearly bounds in with excitement.

"Mama, I found you. I escaped. I am back!" she yells through the doorway. The excitement is lost once she reaches her mother moaning and rocking by the hearth.

Sweetness, and iron, and sweat fills the air. Wisps of hair poking through Mama's nightcap cling to her face. Mary grows silent, lost in curiosity for Mama and concern for the work she seems to be doing.

Tiptoeing, she brings the pail to the great iron stove and fills the kettle just as Mama had asked her to. She feels like her Mama's big girl completing this task, but Mama's sounds make her feel so small. The sounds slow down and shrink as Mama's gaze lands back in the little room and on Mary within it.

"Sweet child. I am glad you are back inside. You might have caught your death out there." She beckons Mary to her arms, her white nightgown folding around her like the wings of a great swan. Kissing Mary atop her head and taking off her frozen bonnet, she coos: "You must be my brave girl. I am afraid Pa won't be back in time with the midwife. So you'll . . . you'll . . ." Her voice trails off as she is overcome again by her moans.

Deep, guttural moans that make Mary wonder what cavern was inside her Mama that made her sound so big.

Mary retreats to her frayed pink quilt spread in front of the hearth. Her fingers reach for the pile of books she had placed there, running her hand over the bumps of the embossed leather of her Bible stories Father Christmas had brought. Beneath this, a book of fairy tales with a jaunty frog and rabbit, and finally, her beloved ABC book with a fluffy mama cat looking sternly at her two kittens. Mary wonders if the baby might like this book, though she would of course want to borrow it back now and again. She brings the pile close to her chest and hugs them, willing herself to escape into their pages as she often did when the nights howled, or when Pa is out on a hunting trip. Tonight is no exception as she thumbs through the pages of her fairy tales trying to engross herself but peeking at Mama over the cover. Hot prickles spread down her arms and legs, melting the last of the Snow Queen's clutches.

The glow of the fire illuminates Mama in her nightgown and cap, white like the storm outside, her gown hanging from her like a billowing ghost mocking her with neat and tidy white bows. Mama's gaze is both there and not there, her face ethereal and foreboding, and her big, terrible rumblings remind Mary of thunderous prairie storms that roll in when the air is hot and sticky. The forks of lightning lash the plains those nights. Mary would shiver under her covers despite the heat and try to sneak a few extra moments of lamplight before being told to say her prayers and stop wasting oil.

Here is Mama now, thunder *and* lightning. Mary curls up with her books again, uncertain how the baby will arrive, let alone how Mama would be tame enough to receive it.

She wonders if the stork will make it through the hurricane of snow and drop the baby through the chimney as Kitty had told her in town one day as she waited on the general store stoop for Mama to finish her groceries. Mary gets the feeling that with all Mama's hard work, it might be more like when Papa helped Babe, the calf, last spring.

The tight feeling in Mary's chest returns. How would she know what to do if Mama needed her?

Spinning thoughts lead to a place of visiting her mother, too beautiful to be buried, lay to rest in a glass casket awaiting her prince.

Mary's heart does not feel brave now. She feels frozen, but from the inside this time. If she can make herself as small and still as possible, the feeling will pass—a church mouse receding to its hole. Mama and baby would just have to be fine without her.

Except . . .

Gerda and Kai would not have cowered. No, they would have saved their Mama from any evil befalling her. Even if they were a little scared.

She draws in a big breath and strides back to her mother, chin lifted.

In her revery, Mary fails to notice the old dog bark, announcing the arrival of the sled, its bells glistening against the opaque wall of snow. Footsteps approach the wooden door.

Pa is home!

He will know how to help. Like a knight saving the princess, Pa will know how to help Mama, their queen, and he'll give Mary orders so she will be useful, as well.

Through the door, her big papa bear saunters through, a white devil from head to toe. On his arm a plump ruddy woman. Mary hesitates but catches the twinkling eyes beneath the white powder. Relief pours through her body like honey from the combs Pa harvested in the summer. Without introductions, the woman begins to unravel wool wraps from her body. A pile mounts so high beside Mary, she has to check to see there was still a body underneath.

"Wendy," Papa marches directly to Mary's mother and plants a firm kiss on her forehead.

"John," Mama speaks in a daze. "You're here. Myna?" She glances toward the door.

"Ay, I'm here, lass," the woman coos, bringing an immediate calm to the little house. "Dinna fash yersel. The darlin wee one will be here soon."

Myna sets about opening her bag. Mary watches her from her mother's side. She remembers Myna in town with her six children. *She must know how babies come*, thought Mary. Upon the table, Myna places torn clean rags and tinctures and herbs Mary had never seen. Sensing her curiosity, Myna beckons the girl over to have a look at the contents.

Mary's fingers gingerly touch a row of bottles standing in rapt attention like the tin soldiers placed neatly in the general store window. Mary reads words like *cramp bark*, *burdock root*, and *black haw*.

Is this medicine to help the baby? Mary wonders. *Or is Myna a witch come to snatch the baby away?*

Mary had already escaped the clutches of the Snow Queen earlier that very day, so she knew no potion would be potent enough to defeat her. She decides her body feels calm around Myna, which means Myna might be trustworthy after all.

Pacing the room, Mama reaches for Pa, who is stuffing his pipe with sweet tobacco. He holds her steady as she walks. Mary wonders if this was what they had looked like in courtship, before they had her and before the weight of working the land had bent them both.

Mama lets out her thunder again, her knees buckle like the weight of it was too much. A shiver runs down Mary's spine, reminding her of her wet clothes, but Mama's sounds make her too afraid to get up and to change.

While Mama was pacing, Myna had placed two chairs side by side, a small pile of rags between them. Mary wonders if one chair is to lay the baby on. But then Mama sits with one side of her bottom on each chair and Myna squats in the middle space, a disciple in prayer, at the base of Mama's nightgown, rising only to place a cool cloth on Mama's neck and squeeze her hand as if to say: "You'll be fine."

Mary rubs her eyes and stares, waiting for the baby. She wonders if Myna would let her sit next to Mama once the baby arrives.

Pa scoops up Mary and brings her in close. She inhales the cold smell of the snow, his tobacco.

"You're soaked to the bone." He sets her down and fetches her flannel nightgown.

Warm contentment permeates her heart when her father wraps his bear paws around her. Sitting at the windowsill, he reads her *The Little Match Girl*, while Mama works hard with Myna and the snow falls all around their house.

"Will Mama be, okay?"

"I am sure of it. And you? You'll be a big sister now. You'll have to be my big brave girl."

Mary nods and buries her face into the breast of Papa's shirt. She knows exactly how brave she can be.

The foreboding white is now a hush over the comfort of their little home. Mary drifts knowing her father has her, the midwife has Mama, and Mama will soon have the baby, and everything is right in the world.

About the Author

Amy Kelly is a former midwife, current family therapist, mother of two, and farmer on Vancouver Island. Her nonfiction appeared in the Yummy Mummy Club (www.ymc.ca), her fiction in 805 Lit + Art, and poetry in *Tiger Leaping Review*. She has been accepted four years in a row to the Yale Writers' Workshop, where she worked with Sarah Darer Littman, LaTanya Mc Queen, and Jacqueline Mitchard. She was selected for the Simon Fraser University Writer's Studio 24/25. Her YA manuscript, *Little Acts of Useless Rebellion*, was second runner-up in the 2023 Leapfrog Press Global Fiction Prize. Her last great adventure was hiking to Everest Base Camp at age forty. She hopes publishing her novels will be her next.

You can find Amy Kelly on:
Instagram @amykellywrites

And visit her website at https://www.amykellyauthor.com/

REVELATIONS IN THE SNOW

Revelations in the Snow

Debby Meltzer Quick

IT HAD BEEN THE FIRST time Peter Reed had stepped out of the monastery in almost four years. He had seen the sun through the stone-rimmed window of his cell but hadn't noticed the way it reflected off the oil slicks on the pavement. The pedestrians rushed by like water running off the mountains into a springtime river. Peter found his body drifting toward the curb, and he had to step back as a plumber's van passed by too closely, the breeze from the movement blowing his long, overgrown hair around his face. It was December in Arizona, and Peter wore a long-sleeved shirt and jeans. Soon, he would be in a place where he would have to wrap himself tight with woolen scarves and gloves, a heavy down jacket, and most likely boots and a stocking cap.

Peter had left more than just the winter season behind when he'd walked away four years earlier. He'd left all of his clothes, his book collection, his keepsakes . . . his family. None of the material items mattered, of course. But he had left behind his wife, his daughter, and his son. They had only been children. Graham was just about to start his senior year in high school, and Kaya would have been a freshman.

He sighed. Kaya. She'd been the reason he had left.

He quickly wiped that thought from his mind.

No, it hadn't been because of Kaya. It had been what Kaya had represented.

She had been having trouble with her best friend that day, and she was feeling sad. She was crying quietly, a single tear softly rolling down her smooth, pink cheek. He had wanted to help her, to make her feel better. He pulled her into his arms as he considered which words would bring her comfort. A thought ran through his head: *I wish I could take all of your pain away. If I could make it different for you, I would. But I just don't have control over it.*

He was working the words around his brain, trying to decide if they were the right ones, but before he could speak, Kaya spoke the words that would change everything for him.

"Control over what?"

Peter dropped his arms and stepped back from their embrace. He knew he hadn't spoken those words out loud. They were only in his head. And that's what terrified him. Because Peter had a secret.

Peter could hear what other people were thinking. It had begun when he was fourteen years old, and he'd thought he was going crazy. What sensible person wouldn't have thought that, though? At first, he assumed he was developing a mental illness, which . . . wouldn't have made him sensible, of course, but it didn't take long for him to figure out that the thoughts he heard were absolutely real.

He had tested it out several times to be sure. One time, he heard a friend's thoughts about going out behind the cafeteria to smoke the joint he had hidden in his bookbag after the final bell. Later that day, Peter mentioned to this friend that he would be interested in getting high, and the friend smiled, bringing out the joint from the pocket of his bag. Peter was also able to figure out which girls liked him, and why, and he used it to his advantage. By senior year, he had been dating Justine Malleck for a year and a half. He was always at least one step ahead of her, finding things to make her happy, and she didn't understand how he did it. Then, right before graduation, he heard her practicing her breakup speech in her head. She was going away to college and didn't want to have a long-distance relationship. Peter got to her first, letting her know that their relationship had run its course and he felt it was time for them to move on. She was stricken, but he could also sense that she was relieved she hadn't had to break his heart. It was a mixed bag; his heart had been broken either way.

But that night, with Kaya's statement, it appeared that his abilities had taken on a new form. Not only could he read others' thoughts, but he could now apparently also share *his* thoughts with others. He was projecting thoughts.

His blood turned cold. How could he explain to his wife and children that, all this time, he'd had inexplicable—magical, maybe? he sometimes wondered—skills that allowed him to read minds, but he had never gotten around to telling them? And what did it mean that his skills were morphing into something new?

He panicked. He had to protect his family.

What if it went beyond mere projection? What if his thoughts became tangible, and he was able to make things happen with only a thought? He remembered the last time Graham had pissed him off with his typical teenager bad attitude. Peter had imagined binding his hands together and throwing him in the closet for an hour. It was just a thought. Parents thought things, imagined things. Good parents *only* thought, though. They never acted on it. But what if . . .

At the time, Peter tried to shake the thoughts out of his head. Maybe it was nothing. Maybe Kaya hadn't heard his thoughts. Maybe it was a fluke. Maybe he had actually muttered his words under his breath but hadn't realized it. He was almost one hundred percent sure this was not the case, but the implications were too high to make any decisions without knowing for sure. So, just like he had when he was younger, he tested his theory.

The next day, he tried three times to project his thoughts to different members of the family, but nothing happened, and he started to feel his anxiety recede just a bit. But the fourth time proved he had the right to be concerned.

He had been sitting on the couch with Kaya, watching a movie. It wasn't a good movie, but Kaya seemed to be enjoying it. She leaned her head against his shoulder and gnawed on salty popcorn. Peter took the opportunity to see if he could project his thoughts.

This movie's really stupid.

And then it happened.

She turned to him with a small smile and and shoved him in the arm. "It's not *that* bad, but it's my day to choose," she said. "You'll just have to deal with it."

Peter's life blood seemed to rush out of his body. It was true then. He could project his thoughts into others. And, perhaps, it was just the beginning of what he could do.

He swallowed down his fear and tried to continue to act normal around his family while he worked to figure out what he needed to do the rest of the night.

Later in bed, Janice tried to catch his eye. "What's going on, Peter?" she asked. "You seem so distant. Is there something going on at work?"

Peter looked up from the book he was staring at but not processing. "What?" he asked. "Oh. Um. Yeah, I've been working on some tough projects. Nothing too bad. I'm just thinking about my plan."

Janice nodded. "We need to have the talk about you leaving your work at the office again, don't we? Peter, you're in advertising. No one will die if you come home and relax, you know." She reached up and started to rub his shoulder. "Your family needs you to be present. You normally are, but for the last two days, you've been somewhere else. Come back, okay?"

Peter forced a smile onto his face. He nodded. "Okay," he said. "I'll try."

Janice grinned. "Great. You can start by scratching my back. I have a nasty itch." She turned away from him, and he reached up to scratch her itch. "Lower."

Peter read her: Janice wasn't worried about him. She just wanted him to be more present, to enjoy his life with his family. Which is what made what he needed to do next nearly impossible.

He didn't pack more than the essentials: a few changes of clothes, his reading glasses, a notebook, two pens, a candid photo of his family, one book, and a wallet filled with cash. He called a cab before he faced them. That way, there would be no turning back.

"I have to go," he said to the surprised look on their faces as he walked toward the door carrying his well-worn travel bag. "It's not because of you. I love you, all of you. This isn't because I've stopped loving you. This is all because of me. I have to . . . figure some things out. I can't explain. I just know I have to do it. I'm . . . I'm so sorry. Janice, I left all of the money in the bank for you and the kids. I know it's not the same as having both salaries, but I'm hoping it can get you by for some time. If you need help, please reach out to my parents. I know they'll help you."

He opened the door as the cab pulled up to the curb.

"I love you all so much." His throat was restricting. "I-I'll miss you so much. I'm so sorry."

He walked out the door and their voices followed him.

"Peter, what's going on? I don't understand!"

"Dad, where are you going? Don't go!"

"Dad, this is crazy! You're just leaving us, just like that? This can't be real."

"Please, Peter. Can't we talk about this? Maybe we can come up with another way . . ."

By the time the cab had pulled away, gotten to the end of the street, and turned the corner, Peter Reed was in tears. The cab driver turned around as he drove. "Are you okay, man?"

Peter nodded but said nothing.

Two months later, after working various jobs as a dishwasher or busboy to make his way, he found himself in Arizona at the monastery. He had asked around and found what he wanted. It was a silent monastery, and for once in his life, Peter wanted silence. Complete silence.

Sometimes, the silence drove him mad. He mostly secluded himself from the monks, not wanting to penetrate their thoughts. He would only come out for meals and to do his chores. He spent his time reading philosophy and ancient texts, trying to figure out what was going on in his mind. He would journal his thoughts every day. Why him? Was he somehow chosen, or was it random? Were there others out there like him, or was he some sort of anomaly, completely alone in his suffering?

The silence eased his constant angst, and he found some peace. In no time, four years had passed. It felt like perhaps just one. Time had become irrelevant, and Peter concluded it was time to face the world once more. He retrieved his few belongings and his leftover cash and walked back through the front door of the monastery.

So there he stood, on the curb in front of the Greyhound station, waiting for the bus that would deliver him back to Wisteria once more, just minutes from his family home, to his unknown fate.

When he arrived in town, he stopped at Target and bought himself appropriate winter clothing. Then he carefully made his way to the library. He had to trudge on foot through the snow. It had been four years since he had even considered snow, but now here it was, same as ever: cold, and slushy under his new, ill-fitting boots. He wrapped his jacket tighter around his shoulders. A woman brushed by, cursing the cold inside her brain, her thoughts available to Peter as if she'd handed them to him on a silver platter. It was taking some time to get used to the noise again. On the bus, he'd had to weed through the internal ministrations of several fellow travelers, including many who wanted to be anywhere but on a bus to their current destinations. There were three who were intoxicated, their thoughts erratic and disturbing. Some slept, and fragments of their restless dreams infiltrated Peter's mind. He'd had to work on mindful breathing, a skill he had picked up from observing the silent monks when he allowed himself to be in their company. He was learning to tune some of the noise down to a dull roar. Otherwise, he would lose his mind.

At the library, he perused the local papers. He found the announcements for the Wisteria High graduating classes for his children. Graham had graduated near the top of his class. Kaya had been head cheerleader her senior year. He found photographs of her team in action and a professional team photo. She had grown so much. She was eighteen now, an adult. She was a freshman at Palmetto State University, where Graham was a senior. He hoped they saw each other on a regular basis. He hoped they were close. He hoped his son was looking out for his sister. He wondered if they each had someone special in their lives. He wondered the same about Janice. He would find out soon.

He stalked them. He didn't mean to. He just couldn't bring himself to approach the door of his own house and ring the bell. What would he even say? "Hi, honey, I'm home!" He snickered. No, he had made his bed already.

He needed more information. He needed to know if they were . . . okay. If they had survived . . . his leaving. He looked at the ground beneath his feet. He wasn't a narcissist, but he knew. He knew it must have been devastating to his wife and children to literally watch him walk out one day, without any warning, and never come home. It was possible they would never want to see him again. And they would be justified.

After the library, he had found a heavy sweater at Goodwill to wear under his puffy down jacket. He invested in some thick wool socks to wear inside his boots. He was starting to get the hang of the cold again. But even in the warmer clothes, he shivered as he watched the house. Christmas was two days away, and his family was getting ready.

Graham and a girl he didn't recognize had come back to the house that afternoon and removed a tied-up fir tree from the top of Janice's station wagon. They brought it into the house, talking and laughing all the while. Peter felt a tug at his heart. Graham had someone special in his life. And ten minutes later, Graham and his girlfriend came back outside, followed by Kaya, her hair obscured by a bright pink beanie with a large pompom on top. Peter held back his laughter. Kaya, always the cheerleader, the center of attention. Then, moments later, a young man came out the door. He scooped up a handful of snow in his gloves, fashioned a snowball, and threw it lightly at Kaya's back. Kaya let out a mock protest and turned around to haul some snow at the boy. Pretty soon, all four of the young people were laughing and tossing snow at each other good naturedly. Then the strange boy took his daughter in his arms and kissed her. A boy was kissing Kaya. And Peter was witnessing it. It was all he could do to stop himself from stepping out from his hiding place and rushing up to the boy to pull him away and give him a piece of his mind.

But then he remembered. That piece of his mind wasn't relevant to these people anymore.

No. Peter was just an observer. An observer of the family he had once made with Janice.

Janice.

After another ten minutes of watching and longing, the door opened once more, and Janice stepped out. And in her hand was . . .

The hand of another man.

Peter could not see who it was. He was tall, about the same age as him, and he was smiling. His hat and scarf were enough to keep his identity a secret, though.

Peter thought he had a right to know. He *had* to know. Who was this man, the man who was holding *his* wife's hand, the hand that legally belonged to him?

But . . . did it anymore? It had been four years. That would have been long enough . . . He would have to return to the library and do some more research. But he was pretty sure that four years would have been long enough for Janice to declare marital abandonment. For all Peter knew, he and as wife might be divorced now. The thought slayed him.

Kaya and her boyfriend were looking toward the house, holding hands. Graham had his arm around the shoulders of his girlfriend. The strange man was still holding Janice's hand, but now he was speaking and pointing at the house. There was an animated discussion that Peter could not hear. Then the man went up to the porch and came back with a box. It was a box of outside Christmas lights. The same box that Peter had wrestled with for many years, returning it to the garage each New Years's Day. The man put the box down on the ground and started to pick up a string of lights. They were tangled. The man smiled and then he took off his hat, and Peter got his first clear look.

Peter gasped.

It was his children's pediatric dentist. What was his name? Dr. Flagg. Steven Flagg. And Peter had actually liked the guy at one point. He'd had a cage full of hamsters in his office for the kids to watch.

Now Peter was dumbstruck. As he watched, the family worked together to untangle the lights. Then Kaya started to sing "Jingle Bells," loudly and poorly. Graham laughed and joined her, and soon everyone was singing. It was the perfect picture of family Christmas joy.

Only it was his family. And he was no longer part of it.

When he had arrived in Wisteria, Peter wasn't sure yet if he would approach that house, and ring that bell, and take the chance to talk to Janice, and Graham, and Kaya, to try to explain, to try to beg their forgiveness, to try, perhaps, to come home, at least in some manner that they could accept. But now, he knew that he would not be ringing that bell, not talking to his . . . family, and he would not be letting them know what had been happening to him for the last few years.

No. That would be selfish.

It appeared that the last thing the people he loved the most needed right now was for him to drop back into their lives.

Their lives were happy, meaningful, and fulfilled, and they would continue to be that way without him. And that's how it would stay.

The next week, Peter was on a plane to Japan. He was not sure what drove him to buy a one-way ticket to Tokyo, but somehow, he was on his way. And every mile took him farther and farther from Wisteria, and the life he had left behind four years ago. But even as he looked toward his time in a foreign country, he was feeling optimistic. He knew he didn't need to worry anymore. It wasn't that Janice, Graham, and Kaya all had found love. It was more that they were still together, still a family. They were supporting each other, helping each other, and were still having fun celebrating the holidays together. They could laugh together, which meant they could probably also cry together and hold each other when times were hard. They had gotten through what must have been the hardest thing they'd ever have to handle—the fact that he had left. And they had survived. Not only survived. They had thrived.

He closed his eyes and let himself drift off into a peaceful sleep, lulled by the constant purr of the jet engines.

It would be four more years before he would lay eyes on his family again.

If you want to learn more about the Reed family and their friends, pick up a copy of **Don't Say a Word**, *book 1 of the Anomaly series, on Amazon, Kindle Unlimited, or Barnes and Noble. Coming soon, book 2 of the series,* **Blinding Justice**.

About the Author

Debby Meltzer Quick is a full-time social worker in Portland, Oregon. She has been writing for fun since age twelve. Growing up in Massachusetts, she became a huge fan of Boston sports, especially the Red Sox and the Patriots, and she aspired to be a sports reporter. She is an avid reader of fiction. She lives with her husband, daughter, two cats, and one rabbit. She has completed two series of seven books each that take place in the fictional city of Eastboro, Massachusetts, in the 1980s: the McKinney High Class of 1986 series and the Anomaly series.

You can find Debby Meltzer Quick on:
Instagram @quickdebby_author
TikTok @dbmquick

And visit her website at https://debbymeltzerquickauthor.com/

WINTER ESCAPE

Winter Escape

Eliza Vaccaro

THE ANTIQUE COO-COO CLOCK behind the ornate front desk of the Queen Anne Inn told us it was 2:00 p.m. as we patiently waited to check in. We'd been anticipating this much-needed winter weekend getaway, and it was finally here! The charming innkeeper, Jake, provided Raven and me an overview of the Inn and the keys to our room, which, we'd learned, had been named after Prince Edward.

We ascended the slightly creaky wooden stairs, which were draped in a rich jewel-toned maroon runner, to our room, eager to discover whether it would look like the enticing images on the inn's website. It did not disappoint. There were two double beds adorned with beautiful blue and white quilts, two windows—with one giving a peek at the ocean—and a lovely bathroom with a huge shower. I could feel the knots in my neck and shoulders gradually loosening, releasing the tension I had been carrying for some time.

"Why don't we unpack and head to tea?" I asked Raven.

"Sounds good to me."

We spent some time talking to the other guests and savoring the blueberry scones that were so warm the homemade clotted cream and strawberry preserves melted into the center. Cucumber and cream cheese sandwiches, fudgy dark chocolate brownies, and shortbread cookies rounded out the teatime offerings.

After satisfying tea, we wandered into the shared living room. I spotted Jake stoking the fire, and I felt overcome with warmth and comfort. I just wasn't sure if it was coming off the fireplace or Jake.

Jake had wavy dark hair, and whenever he turned his head, a strand would fall over his eyes. And those dark eyes with little flecks of amber were mesmerizing. Not that I was looking too closely.

As we passed, he smiled in my direction. He had a nice smile with a slight sweet dimple, and I felt a warm flush across my cheeks that I hoped no one else noticed.

I caught Raven smirking at me.

"What?"

"I haven't seen that look on your face since you were last in love."

"Don't be ridiculous! I was just smiling back at the nice innkeeper."

"If you say so."

I could tell Raven wasn't buying it, and if I'm being perfectly honest with myself, I wasn't sure I was either.

Raven and I were able to get a prime spot on the couch. There were a few couples in the room talking quietly to one another.

As we settled in, I finally had an opportunity to soak in some of the Inn's atmosphere. We were sitting on the couch directly facing the fireplace with a smaller sofa to our right on the diagonal. Several chairs were scattered around the room. The walls were covered in red and gold damask wallpaper, giving the room a warm glow. The floors were dark hardwood and there was an oriental rug just under our feet. Soft fairy lights hung in several corners of the room and a drop-down desk in the corner looked like the perfect place to read or write.

"It's been tough since the breakup with Tom."

"What's it been, six months?"

"Yeah, I just can't seem to stop feeling guilty about breaking up with him. He moved out, but we still have some friends in common, so it just makes it that much harder. I still have him in my Contacts and there has been some occasional texting . . ."

"You didn't tell me that. Is that over?"

"Yes, I don't plan to text with him anymore. I just really need this weekend to clear my head."

"It's okay, Abby. I don't think there's a set timeline for this sort of thing. I think this weekend will be just what we both need."

Raven had just gone through a health crisis, and I knew she still needed some time to heal, too.

She started humming a tune that I just couldn't catch.

"What's that?"

She gave me a big smile and started singing softly, "Let it snow, let it snow, let it snow."

"Well, we can always hope but when we were researching this place, I kept reading in the reviews that it doesn't really snow around here."

"I don't know. It feels like there might be a little magic in the air."

"You have such an imagination."

Raven just gave me a secret smile. I knew that even though she could be quirky, she was more often right than wrong.

Suddenly one of the guests addressed the group.

"I heard it is going to snow up to five inches over the weekend. Did anyone else hear that weather report?"

Maria, one of the staff members, addressed the question. "Oh, it is doubtful we will get any snow, never mind that much. It rarely snows here in Cape Stirling, and when it does it often quickly turns to rain. You might encounter snow ten miles north of here, but it would be a miracle for that to happen here."

The guest just nodded his head and then turned to the woman he was with—I assume it was his wife. He winked and said, "If it does snow, this will be a very romantic weekend for sure." The woman blushed and smiled but didn't say anything.

Although the temperature was dropping, Raven and I decided to get some fresh air. We stepped out onto the porch, and we held our breath at the sight of it. Dusk was descending and the Inn was lit up like a Christmas tree.

"Check out the gingerbread, towers, and wraparound porch!" Raven squealed.

"Wow!" was all I managed to utter.

Along the porch, several welcoming rocking chairs beckoned to me, and I desperately wished it wasn't too cold to sit outside.

"I think I might like to take a little walk around the block and clear my head."

Raven nodded. "Hey, I meant to ask. Who have you been texting?"

"Oh. Just a couple of messages to work."

"You're sure?"

"Raven, yes!"

"Abby!"

"It's just work! Questions about prerequisites for next semester."

"Okay, well, we're leaving work behind this weekend, too, so wrap it up, lady."

"I know, I know. I *need* this break. Let me finish this, and then I'll put my phone away. Okay?"

"Alright. I'm going to go back in and enjoy the fireplace and some hot chocolate with those little marshmallows."

Raven wiggled her eyebrows at me, and I had to laugh.

"You are such a kid sometimes."

As I walked, I felt a knot start tightening in my stomach again. I hadn't been completely honest with Raven. Tom had been texting me. He wanted to get back together, and I knew that would be terrible for me, but he could be hard to resist sometimes.

My phone vibrated then, and I looked down to see it was Tom. But now he was calling.

"Hey, Abby, can you talk?"

I sighed, my breath a small puff in the cold night. "Tom, why are you texting me so much?"

"You know why. I want to get back together."

"We've been through this. I don't think we should get back together." My voice was smaller than it needed to be, but this was a conversation I would've been more comfortable continuing via text messages.

"Come on, Abby, you know you love me."

"I do care about you, Tom," I admitted, kicking at the frozen grass beneath my boot. "But we weren't good together as a couple. We broke up for a reason. I keep telling you we can be fr—"

"I don't want to be *friends*," he mocked. "And you know? I'm starting to think you maybe never loved me."

"Tom, come on, I—"

And he hung up.

The knot in my stomach sunk into a heavy pit of guilt as I slowly, miserably, trudged back to the Inn, tears rolling down my cold cheeks. I hoped to sneak up to the room before Raven or anyone else could see me.

No such luck. Raven was standing on the porch waiting for me.

"Abby, what happened?"

"I didn't tell you everything. I've been talking to Tom. I know I should've made a clean break, but I just felt this pull. Please don't be mad!"

"I'm not mad, but I am frustrated and a little hurt. You could have trusted me to tell me what was going on. I could have helped."

"I know, I know."

"Okay, here's a tissue. Your mascara is running, and you've got that exotic dumpster panda look."

We both cracked up and almost didn't stop until Jake came out on the porch.

"What's going on? It sounds like you're having a good time."

I quickly turned away to make sure I could clean up the makeup before he knew I'd been crying, but it was too late.

"Hey, are you okay?"

"I am. I was just talking with someone who made me upset, but I think everything is okay now. I'm not going to let that person make me feel like that again."

I couldn't read Jake's expression in the dark, but his presence alone was comforting.

"Well, if you need anything, you let me know."

"Thanks, Jake."

"Yeah, thanks, Jake," Raven echoed. I couldn't see her expression in the dark, either, but I knew her well enough to know she was smirking.

The next morning, we woke up around seven thirty. I was determined to put yesterday's conversation with Tom behind me.

I looked out the window hoping there might be snow but . . . nothing. I did see the ocean moving like an icy blue glacier. I shivered at the thought of dipping my toes in there, and then, when the scent of fresh coffee hit me, my thoughts quickly moved to breakfast.

After showering and dressing, Raven and I headed downstairs. The breakfast was set up buffet style and a lengthy line of guests stood patiently waiting to fill their plates. We didn't mind the wait, as it looked like there was plenty of food.

After filling our bellies with French toast stuffed with vanilla mascarpone, sausage from the local farm, and fresh fruit, we were ready to take on the day. We had already planned to go horseback riding.

We saw Jake on the way out. "Heading to the Nobles' stables for a day of riding?"

"Yes, and we can't wait!" Raven replied.

Jake looked at me and smiled. "It will probably be beautiful in the snow."

"I thought that would take a miracle?"

"I have seen a few miracles happen around here. You both enjoy."

Raven and I bundled up and were headed to the car to make the brief drive to the stables.

"Don't you think that was weird?"

"What?" Raven asked.

"What Jake said about the snow."

"Maybe, but don't worry about it. If it snows, it will make everything look festive."

It was a short drive to the stables, and as we parked, we saw a very graceful woman with a blond braid step out of the stables with two majestic white mares. The horses' braids matched each other. The sun was sliding through an opening in the clouds and seemed to light up the woman and the horses in a hazy glow. I shook my head and blinked a few times; it all seemed so ethereal. She introduced herself as Jaimie, and she assisted us with getting acquainted with the horses and helping us get on.

Jaimie said, "Raven, your horse's name is Ella, and Abby, your horse's name is Snowball. I know, I know—my niece, Samantha, had the honor of naming Snowball, so this is how a seven-year-old thinks."

Jaimie was also our trail guide, and we took a slow ride. Pine trees were scattered throughout the forest area, and I found their smell slightly intoxicating. Both horses were very gentle, and we were able to relax on the trail. The tops of my thighs and tip of my nose were cold, but I was enjoying the company of pleasant horses and humans. Jaimie told us about the history of the area as well as the horseback riding business and farm her family had run for several generations.

"My family, the Nobles, have been in this area for more than one hundred years so you could say it is in our blood. Besides the horses, our farm grows a variety of fruits and vegetables, and you might find some of our produce on the local menus. We have a few goats and hens, too. I have my own section of the farm devoted to growing herbs because I use them to create essential oils and some medicinal tinctures that I sell and use in my own practice as a naturopath."

I imagined her life on the farm, a life so different from my own suburban existence. I was fascinated. "You must be busy all the time."

"I'm used to it. The family business is run by all of us, but I am very passionate about helping others with my herbal medicine."

Jaimie then continued with the history of the area.

"Cape Stirling is one of our oldest seaside resorts and named after a British Captain named Stirling who made a few trips here. Pirates used to drop anchor here. There is even a legend that Captain William Kidd left treasure buried here. The area is a protected historic site. Many of our houses and some mansions are now used as inns."

Just as Jaimie was wrapping up her history lesson, I glanced up at Raven and noticed her face was pale and she was leaning in her saddle to one side.

"Raven, are you okay?"

"I-I don't know. I feel weak and exhausted all of a sudden."

Jaimie glanced over her shoulder at us to see what was happening and brought all the horses to a stop with a single command.

We helped Raven off her horse.

We were still in the middle of the trail, and Jaimie quickly tethered the horses to a couple of trees before turning her full attention to Raven.

"I am so embarrassed. I'm sorry. I didn't mean to ruin our ride."

Jaimie reassured Raven, "No worries. I might have something in my backpack here that can help."

"I don't want to be any bother."

"You are no bother. Now, let me look."

As Jaimie rummaged in her bag, I tried to comfort Raven. We weren't the touchy-feely sort of best friends, but surprisingly, she let me wrap my arms around her and hug her tight. Maybe because she wasn't trusting her balance, maybe because she was cold. Either way, I gave her an extra squeeze when she put her head on my shoulder.

"Raven was dealing with Lyme disease a little while ago," I explained to Jaimie, figuring it might help her figure out what to grab from her bag. "They took forever to diagnose it. The antibiotics helped, but now she has chronic fatigue."

"Ugh," Raven groaned into my coat.

"I know it's been rough. Just let Jaimie help you."

I felt Raven nod her head in agreement against my shoulder.

"This is Siberian Ginseng. Have you had it before?" Jaimie asks.

"Ssmph," Raven mumbles into my coat.

"Yes?"

Raven snuck out a thumbs-up without turning her face or moving the rest of her body.

"Okay, so you know that it will help with the fatigue, although it may take a while. I know how to do acupressure. If you want, I can apply pressure on a spot at the top of your head that should also help with the weakness."

Raven agreed to all of Jaimie's recommendations and looked and felt far better once Jaimie was finished with her.

To say I was in awe of this woman would be an understatement. "Jaimie, you are the jack of all trades," I said.

"I have a great-grandmother who was a midwife and what some people called a witchdoctor. Maybe I got the gifts from her."

Raven was moving slowly, but she was able to mount her horse without any help, and once we were riding again, she seemed like her usual self. Though I didn't think I had much control over Snowball, I tried to keep the horse as close to Raven's as I could, just in case she started leaning sideways again.

Suddenly it felt very still and calm. I swear I could "smell snow" coming. It wasn't long after that feeling came over me that we noticed white flakes descending. The snow was light and swirling, and I forgot about being cold.

Jaimie exclaimed, "It's snowing, how exciting! The last time it snowed here was five years ago and it soon turned to rain. It is kind of a miracle."

"Hey, Abby, wasn't that what Jake said this morning? Except it sounded like he knew it was going to happen. Maybe he has psychic abilities."

I rolled my eyes at Raven.

Jaimie asked, "Do you mean Jake at the Queen Anne?"

"That's the one." Raven's smile was big, teasing, meant for me. Jaimie didn't notice, thankfully.

Jaimie said, "Oh, he's a great guy. Good with animals. Good with people. You're lucky to be staying there."

"Don't we know it," Raven agreed, her smile growing to that of a Chesire cat that would probably put the Chesire cat himself to shame.

"I have to admit I was secretly hoping it would snow," I said, desperate for a subject change.

"Me too," Raven agreed.

"I guess I make three!" Jaimie declared.

After our lovely but exhausting horseback ride, we thanked Jaimie and decided to grab a quick lunch at the Marlin Café. We both had tasty, Maryland-style lump crab cake sandwiches and homebrewed, tangy, spiced iced tea. We sat by the window to watch the snow. It was still light, and I wondered if it would just change to rain soon. Raven looked almost like her usual self, and she had some energy to go exploring.

Raven and I spent the rest of the afternoon browsing the shops, and we bought some scented organic candles and a couple of hoodies. The town center was like stepping back in time to the Victorian era. All the shops were lit up with white lights, which made everything feel warmer and more welcoming. The arrival of the snow put everyone in a festive mood. A rich aroma of coffee and chocolate enticed us into a little shop called Enchanted Treats. The aroma that had beckoned us here became even stronger when entering the shop. We couldn't resist. We bought some locally made chocolate truffles and fresh ground coffee.

When we got back to the Inn, snow was still falling lightly, and we were a little wet from our shopping adventures. Once we were warm and dry and had put away our purchases, we headed down to the dining area for tea.

Jake was standing near the bottom of the stairs. He gave me that amazing smile and I felt a tingle run through my body. The weekend didn't have much left to it, but would it be so bad to get to know one another better?

"How was your horseback ride?"

"Well, I was pleasantly surprised it snowed."

Jake said, "I knew it would."

"How could you be so sure?"

"I have lived here all my life. You get a feeling about these things."

"But don't you think this will turn to rain?"

"I don't. I think the snow will start to become heavier and we will get a few inches at least. As our guest said, it will make everything more romantic."

I swallowed hard. *Oh boy.*

Jake accompanied us to the dining room, where we discovered that the day's tea was extra special with chocolate-covered strawberries and what looked like mini ganache cakes.

I'm sure Jake saw my eyes pop when I noticed them, because he explained, "The dessert that looks like ganache is actually a budino, a type of Italian pudding. I think you will enjoy it."

Raven and I sighed a few moments later when we tasted the budino.

"That's amazing!" We both said at the same time and then just started giggling like schoolgirls.

"I think you are both on a chocolate high. I am glad you are enjoying it," Jake said, clearly amused, before wandering over to another table of guests to check on them.

After tea, we agreed to move to the communal living room to relax and enjoy the fireplace and company. As we passed Jake, now at the front desk, I overheard him explaining to one of the guests how to operate the safe in her room.

"Yes, it should open when you enter your code."

"Well, it isn't working!" The guest was exasperated.

"No worries. How about I come up to your room and take a look? I'm sure we can figure it out together." He gave her a smile and opened his arm wide in the direction of the staircase.

The guest visibly relaxed and she led the way. I caught Jake's eye as they passed us, and he winked quickly before the guest turned back to speak to him.

After some time in the living room, I couldn't help but notice that Jake had returned. The other guests started to drift off to their rooms to plan for the evening ahead, and eventually it was just Raven, Jake, and me. Raven excused herself to go to the bathroom and then quietly went upstairs. I didn't mind, as Jake and I had fallen into an easy, relaxed conversation. We found out that we both loved to travel and cook and had a soft spot for anything furry. He then suddenly said, "I want to show you something."

I gave him a doubtful look.

"Come on, it's nothing bad."

He directed me toward the porch. As we stepped outside, I saw a creature move by my feet. I jumped, and Jake let out a deep laugh.

"It's just Samson, our resident cat. He has never seen snow, so he must investigate, but he doesn't venture further than the porch. He knows he has the best meals here."

I could see now that Samson was a very well-fed tuxedo cat.

Meow? It sounded like a question. He looked up, and I saw that he had one green eye and one hazel eye.

"Hey, I've never seen a black and white cat with two different-colored eyes."

"Samson is unique, but he would have to be to fit in around here."

Samson was also friendly and rubbed up against my leg. It felt like a little lion giving me his royal blessing. He then quickly headed to his heated cat house to get warm.

Once Samson was tucked in, I noticed that it was still snowing. The snow was coming down heavy now in big fluffy flakes, but I wasn't cold, even without our coats. Suddenly the clouds parted in the night sky and some stars revealed themselves.

Jake gently took my hand while he pointed out the stars. I felt my heart leap into my throat, and I was glad it was dark since the heat radiating off my cheeks told me I was blushing the color of a ripe cherry tomato.

Raven and I slept in a little bit later after such a busy day.

"So, tell me everything."

"There is nothing to tell."

"I don't believe that for one minute!"

"Okay, okay. We talked, we went out on the porch, and we held hands while we looked at the stars."

"Very sweet!"

"Oh, stop it! It was no big deal."

"If you say so, Abby, but I think it might be something special."

I just smiled and hoped she was right.

Jake was still smiling at me this morning when we went downstairs, which was a good sign. We arrived for the late breakfast so there weren't as many other guests present. Raven and I ate lightly since we were going for massages.

Jake said, "It snowed several inches overnight, but since you are walking to the spa, I don't think you will have any trouble. I look forward to seeing you later."

Our boots crunched through the snow as we made our way to the spa. We were greeted at the spa with a lovely, calming aroma and sent to our respective treatment rooms. After the horseback riding, it was good to have some of the kinks rubbed out. I found, as the masseuse worked, that instead of the feelings of guilt I had been carrying around ever since ending things with Tom, that my thoughts drifted toward the charming innkeeper and his smile; to the way the sun worked its way through the branches on the riding trail yesterday; to Jaimie's history lessons and tinctures; to the way Raven leaned on me, trusting me and our years of friendship to take care of her when she needed me. The weekend had been passed quickly, but it'd served its purpose: I'd gotten out of my own head.

After our massages, our hair made it seem like we had a great fright, but it was worth it to feel as if I were wrapped in a warm blanket of contentment.

Raven asked, "Look, all teasing aside, what do you think about Jake?"

"I'm not sure but he does give me the tingles."

Raven smiled. "That sounds like a good start."

I smiled back. I had to agree that Jake and I might be a good start. We were checking out tomorrow morning, but maybe I'd ask for his number and see where that took us. After all, according to the locals, we'd witnessed a miracle with the snow falling this weekend, so that had to be a good sign that something special was in the works.

About the Author

Elizabeth "Eliza" Vaccaro is an RN writer who has written numerous clinical education documents for a past employer. She has recently decided to venture into the world of fiction with her short story, "Winter Escape." Eliza currently lives outside of Charleston, South Carolina, but is still a Jersey Girl at heart and can't understand why anyone would want to pump their own gas!

You can find Eliza Vaccaro on:
Instagram @eliza.vaccaro

SNOWFLAKES & SECOND CHANCES

Snowflakes & Second Chances

Krista Renee

Chapter 1

Lulu

IF YOU WANTED SNOW DURING "winter," Texas was not the place to be. We'd have black ice at the most. If we got really lucky, we'd get a light dusting in April. This had been the case since I'd been born. I guess the weatherman didn't get that memo.

My bare legs sank into two feet of snow when I stepped off the porch. It was pushing seventy yesterday. Now it couldn't have been more than twenty. Thank goodness it was Saturday and I didn't have to go to town. Texans were good at a lot of things—barbeque, big hair. We weren't good at driving in the snow. Heck, we didn't even own snow tires.

"I'm dragging Lu to golf, Momma H," Ella said from inside. Apparently, she hadn't gotten the memo either.

I ran my fingers along my arms. The temp was dropping, and fast. If it kept up, we'd be snowed in.

"What. The. F—?"

"It's snow!" I peered over my shoulder. Guess she got the memo.

She rolled her eyes with a set jaw. "I see that, Luella. Why is it here?"

"Oh, you're mad-mad, you're using my full name," I said with a smile. "And it's here because it's January fifteenth." Her pouty shocked face may have been my favorite thing I'd seen all day. Then again, it was only ten in the morning.

"No. This is Texas. It's not supposed to be here." She threw her head back and whimpered. Legit whimpered. "I wanted to go golfing."

"Can't you do that on your phone?"

She rested her arm on my shoulder and gestured to the white blanket. "I can do lots of things on my phone. Golfing isn't one of them."

"We could make hot cocoa," I suggested. "And watch *Titanic*. Nothing says romance like your love sinking to the bottom of the sea."

"Actually," she started. She pulled me back inside the house. "Lots of things say romance. No shade to Leo, he's hot and all, but he's not my idea of a good time. Just like this snow wasn't part of my plan."

My lips pressed to her cheek while my fingers played with the diamond ring on my left hand. "You're adorable, all pouty. It's making me want to call the weatherman and ask if we can keep it a bit longer."

She buried her face in a pillow on the couch with her butt literally in the air. Good lord, my future wife was more dramatic than I was. If she kept it up, she was gonna carry our babies. I walked around the couch and put her head in my lap.

After a long sigh, she turned and met my eyes. My heart pounded when she eventually smiled. We'd been a couple almost a year come February, but every time she looked at me was like the first time. It didn't matter that we'd known each other since second grade.

"I was supposed to beat you at golf, then we were supposed to go look at venues. News flash, sugar, we can't do that while Frosty pays us a visit." She groaned when she looked at the melted slush at my feet. After a heavy sigh, she grabbed a towel from the guest bathroom and tossed it at me. "Friggin' Frosty."

Chapter 2
Ella

I WAS MARRYING LULU ANABETH Hutchinson in three months and two days. Before that happened, I was making it my personal mission to beat her at golf before we walked down the aisle. For the past two months, she'd made a hole in one almost every time we played. I was going to beat her, dang it.

Momma smiled at me while she made a pie. "You look nice."

"I'm dragging Lu to golf, Momma H." And I was going to win.

A blast of igloo cold hit me in the face when I stepped outside. So many things were wrong with the picture in front of me. The first being Luella was wearing shorts and a cami. The second being it had friggin' snowed overnight. Nobody was gonna have a good day because it snowed, least of all me. I brought my arms across my chest and shot daggers at the back of her head. "What. The. F—?"

"It's snow!" Her smile was almost warm enough to make me forget it was, like, zero degrees.

My fiancée, everyone, was a genius. I rolled my eyes. "I see that, Luella. Why is it here?"

Going from the extreme cold to the extreme heat when I drug her inside made the tips of my fingers tingle. I flopped on the couch with a whimper. She put my head in her lap. No matter how bad my mind wanted to stay angry, her being made my body relax.

"We have time, doctor."

"Three months is hardly time, Lu."

Her fingers ran through my hair. I pressed my lips to her inner wrist.

"I'm gonna marry you, doctor. It doesn't matter where. I'm marrying you. We don't get snow that often, though. I say we get dressed in warm clothes and go camping. We can watch the sunrise as fiancées and fall asleep in each other's arms."

My brow cocked. I sat up and rested a knee on either side of her. "Will that make my future wife happy?"

Her eyes lit up when she smiled. "Very."

"Fine. We'll go frigging camping. Promise me once the snow goes away that we'll get serious about picking a venue."

"There's nothing more I want in the world, Doctor Eleanor Lennox Young."

Summer in Texas sucked, but winter might have it beat. But I'd take a million winters if it meant seeing Lu wearing a beanie and scarf. Sweet lord, she was adorable, and somehow I'd convinced her to marry me. The strongest woman I knew was going to be my wife.

After setting up the tent, I walked behind her and wrapped my arms around her. I buried my nose in her hair and inhaled. "How in the world did I get so lucky?"

She turned to face me. Her fingers fixed my beanie before moving to play with my scarf. "After everything we've been through, I'd say we're both pretty damn lucky. We're a team. We're in this together."

Cold wind hitting my face mixed with her kneeling on one knee, made my cheeks, fingertips, and tips of my ears heat.

"Ella, you were my first everything, but I wasn't ready. We needed to go through Freddy before we were ready for us, before I was ready. I'll never feel the same about anyone else as I do about you. You're my person. My reason. The ice cream on top of my pie. I could do life without you, but I don't want to. I want to sit with you on Momma's porch when we're eighty, sipping tea. I want everything with you. Will you marry me? I can't promise it'll be chaos free, but at least it'll be a fun ride."

I didn't realize tears streamed down my face until the wind hit me a second time. She would propose during a snowstorm. "It's snowing."

She smiled. "It's better than your proposal while your fingers were on my—" I shot her a look before she finished her sentence

Christ. She was never gonna let that go. "Touché, sugar."

"Will you?"

I nodded and helped her to her feet. "Duh."

She threw her arms around my neck with a squeal. My hands went to her waist seconds before I lost my footing and tumbled onto white powder. Unfazed that we were on the wet ground, her lips pressed all over my face. "She's gonna marry me!"

"You realize I was already gonna marry you, right? That's kind of why *I* proposed."

She rolled her eyes. "Yeahhhhh, but I wanted a proposal, too. Who says girls can't have two proposals?"

As far as snow angels went, the one we unintentionally made will always be my favorite.

Chapter 3
Lulu

THE TIPS OF MY FINGERS were numb as I sipped the gas station coffee Ella got me. It would've been practical to huddle under our sleeping bag, but the way she held me made me forget about practicality.

"I'm enjoying this more than I should," I said while her lips pressed along the curve of my neck.

"Frozen coffee or warm kisses?"

I smiled as I turned my head to meet her mouth. "This. All of it. You and me. And I really like being held."

"Lucky for you, I like holding you. Granted, I'd like it more if it wasn't in subzero temps."

My fingers wrapped around her neck to bring her mouth to mine. "Are you complaining, doctor?"

"No, ma'am."

"Good. Keep kissing me until my face warms up."

Chapter 4
Ella

I WOKE UP SHIVERING THE next morning. Even with Lu beside me, the chill in the air was miserable. Bone-chilling miserable. If I'd had the energy, I'd blow my breath to see if it froze.

How Lu managed to stay asleep was one of the greatest mysteries of the universe.

She buried her face in my chest with a whimper that made me tighten my numb fingers around her waist. "Ella, tell Elsa to go away."

"I thought you were Team Snow yesterday."

She winced and snuggled closer. "That was before I woke up to every part of my body aching. Why is it so cold? This is not romantic at all."

"I hate to say I told you so, buttt I kind of did."

My head hit the frozen ground when she yanked my pillow from under me and whacked me in the face with it. "Shut up."

She threw her stiff denim-covered leg over my hip. "Every part of my body hates me."

"That's because it's zero degrees, and you *wanted to go camping*."

"I thought it would be romantic. What the hell is this?"

"Cold," I said with a smile. Being right would never fail to give me a tiny bit of glee.

"Yeah, friggin' duh. I resent my statement. I no longer want to marry you."

"My ice heart sheds a tear."

After a long silence, she looked at me. "Can we go home? I wanna take a shower and warm up."

"Only if you say I was right."

I didn't have to be looking at her to know she rolled her eyes. "You're a dick."

"Maybe so, but I was a right dick."

"Marriage proposal rescinds in 3, 2, 1. Say you were right one more time."

I smiled and tilted her chin. "I was right."

She growled and buried her face back in my chest. "I'm cold."

As much as I could do this 'til the cows came home, her safety would always be more important, even if the only danger right then was just her being cold and uncomfortable. "Okay, sugar, let's go home."

Chapter 5
Lulu

THE COLD FRIGGIN' SUCKED. EVEN when we were in Ella's car with the heater on, the cold followed. It had seeped deep into my bones until I was convinced it would stick around forever. My knees rested against my chest. "We're never going in the cold again."

She brought my hand to her lips and kissed it. "Whatever you say, Mrs. Young."

My brow cocked. "I'm taking your last name now?"

"Not if you don't want to. Honestly, I'm just shocked this is the life I get to live."

"Pull over, Ella."

We were already going at a snail's pace. It took a few minutes, but she pulled to the side of the road. After climbing across the console, I sank my knees on either side of her.

Her lips pressed to mine with a soft whimper. She ran her fingers up my back and tangled in my hair. I'd never be able to soak up enough of her. I'd always crave more.

"Our life is pretty dang great, Mrs. Hutchinson-Young. Now, let's go tell Momma I said yes to your proposal."

Chapter 6
Lulu

THE HOUSE SMELLED LIKE CRYSTALLIZED sugar, blueberries, and lemons when we got home. It was the same house I'd lived in since I was born, but something was off. Ella kissed my neck, but I shoved her away.

"Where's Momma?"

Ella pulled me against her and resumed kissing my neck. "Does it matter? We're warm."

"She wouldn't leave a pie in the oven. Ever."

I ran upstairs and barged into her room just in time to see Ella's mom—a.k.a., my future mother-in-law, a.k.a., the woman Ella couldn't stand, which meant I couldn't stand her by proxy—coming out of Momma's bathroom wearing nothing but Momma's silk pink robe that I had given her for Christmas.

My fingers dug into my thighs.

Ella's mom looked at Momma like they'd been doing this for a while. Momma smiled at her and opened the covers for her. As if being snowed in and then half frozen in a tent wasn't enough, I had to catch Momma in bed with my future mother-in-law.

"Is everything okay, Lu?" Ella asked as she appeared beside me and wrapped her arm around my shoulders.

The only thing I could do was squeak as I gestured toward the bed and our moms.

"Oh, my god . . . Mother?"

Lulu and Ella are the main characters in Krista Renee's debut novel, *Bad Idea Lane*, which released in 2024. To read more about them, pick up a copy today! Available in print and ebook on Amazon and other retailers.

About the Author

Krista Renee writes sapphic romances ranging from sweet and sassy to dark and gritty. Her debut novel *Bad Idea Lane* came out in July of 2024, and she's currently working on a dark *Wizard of Oz* retelling. She lives in East Texas. When she's not obsessing over Broadway, she's hanging out with her four munchkins.

You can find Krista Renee on:
Instagram @kristareneeauthor
Facebook @kristareneeauthor

THE WINTER GAMES OF SOPHIE BERLIN

The Winter Games of Sophie Berlin

Renata Illustrata

Game

"REMEMBER, GIRLS, IN TENNIS, 'LOVE all' means neither player has the advantage." Sophie Berlin took a deep breath and blew blonde bangs out of her eyes. The grip felt at home in her hand, her swing a song played from deep muscle memory. "To begin, both players start at 0-0. That's why the first serve is so important."

A crowd of sixteen-year-old girls stood on the side of the tennis court inside a large indoor tennis pavilion watching their teacher. The pavilion appeared old but still posh, with large wood beams on the tall, pitched ceiling and a viewing balcony on one side.

Sophie's tall, slender frame had a hint of curves, and her golden hair complemented lovely hazel eyes. "The first serve shows the other player who you are. So today we're going to work on strategic openings. After that, the most important thing I can teach you about tennis is how to recover after you've made a bad choice in a match, and use the disappointment to refocus your energy."

An auburn-haired girl named Rebecca laughed. "Sounds kind of like dating."

Ainsleigh Vandersloot, standing next to her, whispered, "Like I'd *ever* take dating advice from someone who's thirty."

Sophie smiled. "I heard that Ainsleigh."

"Sorry, Ms. B."

"Let's start with you then. C'mon. Over here. Show me your opening serve."

Ainsleigh snorted then reluctantly took her position behind the baseline. The girl fidgeted with her hair and adjusted her tennis skirt while everyone waited.

"Ainsleigh," said Sophie, "your opponent is not going to hold play while you adjust your ponytail or pull down your skirt."

The girl rolled her eyes. "Ms. B., what twisted fifty-year-old businessman even invented tennis skirts anyway? I feel like I'm wearing one of those trampy Halloween costumes."

"That's an excellent question, Ainsleigh. How would you like to spend winter break researching the origin story of tennis skirts and writing a report about their provenance?"

"No way! Ski trip."

"Well, then, let's get back to practice. Watch me." Sophie hit a flat serve with a resounding *pok* of her racket. The sound echoed off the expanse of the pavilion as the ball torpedoed to the other side of the net and slammed to its target: deuce court.

Vandersloot clapped. "Wow, Ms. B.! You're in pretty good shape for someone *your* age."

And that was a gut punch, Sophie thought. *But nothing can shake my good mood today, not even Vandersloot. I am hours away from winter break and my three-day tournament—step one in my plan to start my own tennis camp one day.*

Sophie's cheeks were sore from constant smiling. Months and months of planning had led up to this.

Sophie grabbed another ball and handed it to her student. "Now you try."

Ainsleigh threw the ball in the air and smacked it with her racket behind a guttural grunt, but the ball fell just short on her side of the net.

"That's okay, Ainsleigh. We'll keep working on it. Rebecca, can you show us your best flat?"

Rebecca assumed the position, pitched the ball in the air, whacked it across the net, and watched it come down just on the wrong side of the sidelines. The girl deflated. "Fault."

"It's long but that's okay, Rebecca. I love your power! We just need to work on your control. Your serve has come a long way this semester. Awesome job."

"Girls, it took me years of practice to nail my opening serve. You'll get there. Work hard, don't get distracted, and I promise your game will improve."

At day's end, Sophie locked up Tarlington Tennis Pavilion and made her way to her old Volvo in the staff parking lot, her court shoes crunching the snow beneath her feet. She drove out past the school's imposing wrought-iron entrance gate embossed with *Foxcroft Academy, East Aurora, New York, est. 1933.*

She shook her head. *Foxcroft, really? It's like something a Brontë sister would dream up.* Sophie had come to Foxcroft a year earlier from another school, the exclusive private academy being closer to where she lived, and though it was undeniably a little pretentious, she couldn't deny the exceptional pay. Foxcroft gave her a full-time position monitoring study hall in the mornings and tennis instruction in the afternoons because the academy also needed a coach for their tennis team, the East Aurora Silver Foxes.

Cracking the window, she took a deep breath of icy December air. Sophie lived in an apartment complex with very neat grounds and landscaping, but all the buildings were practically indistinguishable. She still loved her apartment because it had two roomy bedrooms, they allowed pets, and it also sat a few blocks away from East Aurora's tennis club.

Thirty minutes later, Sophie sat at her kitchen table in panda bear footy pajamas hard at work on a to-do list. The jazzy sophistication of Billie Holiday played in the background. Billie's sad tone always reminded Sophie of her mother.

Now that this term's behind me, I can just worry about the tournament . . . so much to do . . . details overload. What would civilization do without lists? I think it's one of our greatest achievements, right after gelato. It's definitely what separates us from the animals.

Right on cue, her cat, Constance, a haughty Siamese, jumped onto the table.

"Constance, you naughty diva! You know Anna doesn't allow you on the table." She transferred the cat to her lap and, after a few mutually satisfying strokes, returned to her list-making. She became so deep in thought she didn't even hear her roommate enter the apartment.

A tall brunette with pale skin and deep-brown eyes entered the kitchen. "Hey, girl, what're you doing? Oh, that looks like one of Sophie Berlin's famous to-do lists. Can I see that?"

Sophie handed her the paper and watched Anna scribble something on it. Anna passed it back. She'd written, *14. Do something that's not on a list!*

Sophie took it back. "Hah. That list is for the tournament. You're off tomorrow, right?"

"Yes, I'm off, and I'm driving to the printer's and picking up the tournament flyers to foist upon innocent members of the public, dragging them out of their homes and vehicles, if necessary."

Sophie turned the page to start a new list.

Anna poured her a glass of wine. "Soph, you know as the tournament chairperson you can delegate some of this. Has that cat been on the table again?"

Sophie did not look Anna in the eye. "I can neither confirm nor deny the allegation." She rose and soaped up a dishrag then cleaned the table. "Besides, Anna, I gave you a handful of things to do."

"I meant like the other people volunteering. That's what volunteers are for."

"I'm letting you help because I trust you. I appreciate the volunteers, but I don't trust them."

"Okay, boss lady. Well, I had a rotten day at work, so I thought I'd make my mom's pasta carbonara tonight. Sound good?"

"It sounds like heaven. You're a saint."

"I'm pretty sure there's no Saint Anna who's a gay physical therapist."

"Well, there should be," Sophie said, helping herself to more wine. "You work at a children's hospital rehabbing sick kids—that sounds like a saint to me."

"Last week I snuck into the imaging room and screamed into an MRI machine to stop myself from punching a doctor." Anna opened the fridge and filled her arms with ingredients.

"Well, I may have *accidentally* whacked Ainsleigh Vandersloot in the head with a slice serve last week."

"*Accidentally?* I call b.s. You never miss."

"I don't think you needed an MRI for valid medical reasons either."

"Take comfort where you can get it, is what I say."

Once the carbonara hit the table, the two girls quickly dug in, falling into happy silence as they savored the thick, unctuous sauce, which clung to the chewy pasta and pancetta. A golden egg yolk dissolved over the salty and creamy concoction, and the entire kitchen smelled of pan-fried pancetta and nutty Parmesan.

"Is it unladylike to lick the bowl?" Sophie asked, surveying her empty plate.

"I'm sure in some cultures it's considered a compliment to the chef. Although I'd like to point out that even your cat doesn't lick her bowl clean." Anna motioned toward the dainty cat bowl in the corner marked with the word *diva* in calligraphy, which had incriminating remnants of crusty, congealed cat food.

"Yep, Constance has a proud stomach. Beautiful creatures think the rules don't apply to them. Let's take the rest of the wine to the sofa. I've got more to-do listing."

Anna groaned but rose and followed her into a cozy den with a large picture window lined with plants and a dark blue, cushy sofa and side chair. After a few minutes of intense scribbling by Sophie and contemplative wine consumption by Anna, Anna looked over at Sophie.

"You know you haven't had a man in your bedroom since that guy came to fix the air-conditioning two summers ago."

Sophie's pen froze. "Where did that come from?"

"I was just contemplating what may happen to you someday when Taran and I are off exploring the Mediterranean in a yacht."

"Why worry about that? You don't have a yacht. Didn't you get seasick that time your staff appreciation party was on a boat last spring?"

"I'm serious, Soph. I'm proud of you for pursuing your dream—this tournament. I really am. Everyone at the hospital's excited about it. You've worked incredibly hard after work every day training the kids who are competing. And it's a great steppingstone toward a tennis camp."

Sophie clinked wine glasses with her.

After taking a sip, Anna continued. "It's amazing, but . . . you're allowed more than one dream."

"Well, when was the last time *you* had a man in your bedroom?"

"I think 2008, and can I say, *eww*? I came out to my mother the next day. I bought her favorite cinnamon soymilk latte and wrote 'Mom, I'm gay' on the cup."

"You're kidding?"

"No. My mother said, 'Honey, I think you picked up the wrong drink. This one's for somebody named Momimgay.' The wrong latte was the least of her problems that day."

"Wait a minute, I think I'm remembering this story now. Was this when we were in college?" asked Sophie.

"Yep."

Constance pranced into the den with a plaintive *meooooow*, then began to preen herself.

"Anna, have you talked to your mom lately?"

"Last week."

"How'd it go?"

"You know, not too bad. She asked me to come home for Christmas, but I told her I had a few shifts over the holidays so we're trying to get a New Year visit together."

"That makes me really happy. I love your mother, if only for her carbonara recipe. What about Taran? Given any thought to introducing her to your mom?"

Anna held up her hand. "Whoa! It's too soon to think about that. We've only been dating a few months."

"I think she's great. And I can't believe you found someone so exotic in upstate New York."

"Welsh isn't that exotic."

"It's exotic for East Aurora. She's well-traveled, speaks three languages, smart, pretty. I could go on."

"Yeah, I hit the jackpot a little bit, which should be proof to *you* that if someone puts themselves out there enough, something good might happen. Remember that guy . . . Reggie? He was nice."

"Yeah, exceptionally nice until after he'd showed me off to all his friends in a 'look at this shiny new thing I got' kind of way, but when I told him, 'It's important to me that you come to my tournaments,' he showed up once and left before it was over. Then came Chris—"

"Wait a minute. If we're going to run down your entire list of dating disasters, I'm gonna need to stretch out on the couch and get comfy." She poured herself another glass of wine, plumped a few pillows, then stretched back. As soon as she did, Constance jumped up and stretched out on her belly. "Well now that we're *both* comfy, you may proceed. I think you were on . . . who was it? . . . Chris? Is he the one that looked like a beach lifeguard?"

Sophie pointed a finger at Anna. "I know, right? Sometimes I suspected him of spray-tanning. Yuck!"

"And you dated Beach Lifeguard right before we graduated?"

"Yep. And speaking of which, when I told him I was graduating with honors, he said, 'Cool.' Even worse, I overheard him talking to one of our friends and Chris was saying my major was P.E. and our friend said, 'No man, your girlfriend's getting a double major in Coaching and Athletic Administration.' He didn't even know what my major was."

"Okay, that's pretty bad. In college, your major's like your last name. Sophie, could you add getting your best friend another glass of wine to your to-do list?"

Sophie shook her head but got up and poured her another glass. "So, I realized I'd been dating him for six months and I don't think he ever listened to a thing I said, and he kept wanting to pick out my clothes for me—super revealing ones—that felt kind of creepy."

Anna laughed. "Nobody's perfect, Sophie." Anna lifted her head to take a sip of wine and Constance *meooow*ed indignantly. "I'm sorry I slightly jostled you, Your Majesty. Sophie, you're a beautiful girl. Of course guys will be attracted to that, and yeah, superficial guys might only be attracted to that. Those guys were just self-centered jerks, and you can't expect men like that to be super-supportive of your career. But that doesn't prove there aren't good ones out there."

"I don't know. I guess over time you get one disappointment and then another and another, and at some point, it becomes . . . not worth it. It's easier to stay in your own bubble." Sophie stared into her glass of wine for a few moments.

"Soph, how's your mom?"

Sophie tossed her to-do lists onto the side table. "She's always good.

I talked to her yesterday. I told her I'd come spend the night with her Christmas Eve. She loves the holidays. I love my mom, but, you know, everything's fine if we avoid talking about my father."

"Or he doesn't throw a temper tantrum? You know that's just their relationship, right? It doesn't mean that's the one you'll have, but I get it, you didn't exactly have a great role model for healthy relationships."

"Yeah, I never had to watch soap operas growing up. I had a front-row seat. . . . I think I'm going to have an early night. I have several tournament sponsors to schmooze tomorrow."

"'Night, Soph."

Sophie scooped up Constance from Anna's stomach, and they both headed to her bedroom.

The next day was frantic. Sophie had stops all over town to thank sponsors and pick up checks and brand banners they wanted posted in "prominent spots" at the tournament. The first stop was Edmunds Financial Planning Services where people with lots of disposable income went for investment advice and to plan their retirements.

Sophie walked into Mr. Edmunds's office to find an impressive row of windows that gave a view of downtown East Aurora. Mr. Edmunds was a tall, sixty-year-old with a bald head and triangular jawline. He rose from his seat and shook Sophie's hand. She could feel his eyes crawling all over her like a bad rash.

"Ah, Sophie. It's so good to see you again. I have the check for your charity right here."

"Wonderful! As you can imagine, I do have a lot of stops today but let me tell you once again how much I appreciate your donation. These funds go directly to the new burn ward at Children's Hospital. Also, the children competing in the three-day tournament are public school kids who don't get to play tennis very often so it's a great experience for them, as well."

"Yes, yes. All good things." Mr. Edmunds held out the check. "You know, Sophie, I'd love to take you out sometime."

In her peripheral vision, she could see the family photo on the desk behind him. *Oh, how I'd love to rip this check into a million pieces and scatter them over his head. But remember, it's for the tournament, and thanks to this schmuck, you can help more kids.*

Sophie took the check from his hand and flashed him a big smile. "I'd love to get together with your family some time. Have your wife call me." And she breezed out of his office.

As she returned to her car, she was silently thankful that one large donation had come in anonymously. That would be one fewer ego she must stroke. Mr. Muller, the owner of the East Aurora Tennis Club, was allowing her to host the event at his club and someone had given him a large private donation to cover early expenses.

As the evening wore on, she visited the Regency Group, a realtor development company, and Elite Day Spa, where East Aurora ladies went for massages and the occasional Botox touch-up. Sophie reminded herself that all the schmoozing would be worth it for the children's hospital. However, a few times throughout the day, she did take a second to imagine herself playing a drinking game and taking a gulp or a shot every time she heard the words *dynamic partnership* or *branding opportunity*. By the time she climbed into her Volvo at the end of the day, mentally exhausted, all she wanted to do was drive home and soak in a bath with a glass of wine.

Her phone rang. "Hey, Anna, I'm just about to head home. What's up?"

"I'm just giving you an update: I passed every flyer out to members of the unsuspecting public today."

"Thank you. Oh, I have to tell you that dreadful Edmunds guy came on to me again. I feel like I need to walk through a carwash. Weren't we just talking last night about shallow men who can't commit?"

Anna laughed. "Oh, he can commit alright. Just not to his wife."

"Hold on a sec, a text is coming in. It could be about the tournament."

With an exasperated sigh, she looked at the message and read:

Dear Customer,
We at Order of Play Sports regret to inform you that your sixteen Wilson Pro tennis rackets are on back order and not expected to ship until after December 25th. We apologize for any inconvenience.

"Inconvenience? Anna, I have to have those rackets! The tournament is ten days away! They were paid for by a sponsor and special-ordered a month ago as gifts to the kids playing in the tournament. You know how hard they're working, and they deserve to use those rackets in the tournament. My bath will have to wait. I'm driving over to Order of Play right now!"

"Woohoo! Kick some capitalist butt! I don't think it counts against your karma if you strike a blow against big business."

Set

SOPHIE DROVE INTO THE PARKING lot at Order of Play Sports on a high boil. The sleek and modern sports shop had large panes of glass along the front with a high-end industrial aesthetic. She'd had plenty of time on the drive over to rehearse scathing arguments. Relieved to see the store wasn't closed yet, she opened the door to a bell jingle. Inside, the store was divided in neat sections with dynamic displays including a hang glider suspended on steel cables from the high ceiling. A tall man stood behind the counter with his back to Sophie, restocking a display of water bottles.

Sophie tapped on the counter. "Excuse me."

The man turned. "Yes, may I help you?"

"I'd like to speak to the manager."

"I'm the owner, ma'am—"

"Oh, even better! I'm running the tennis tournament for Children's Hospital. And I received a text that my rackets, which were ordered a month ago, were not yet here—"

"Trust me, ma'am—"

"This isn't about trust. It's about integrity—delivering what you promised. This charity event is not only important to *me*, but it will also benefit child burn victims. I need the rackets—"

"Listen, our ordering system sends out those emails automatically. I'm sorry you—"

Sophie, now on a roll, wasn't about to let him break her rhythm. "Unfortunately, the kids who signed up to compete in this tournament, who've been preparing and practicing for weeks, can't hit balls with apologies, nor do I have a use for them. It's unacceptable to disappoint children who will benefit from this event, who need serious medical treatments."

The man held up his hands in surrender. "I totally agree with you. That's why I drove two cities over this morning to pick the rackets up myself from the warehouse. They're all here and loaded into my car." He pointed to a black Land Rover outside. "I'll deliver them personally to the tennis club first thing in the morning."

Sophie felt the creeping hand of humility reaching over and trying to cover her big mouth. Finally, she said, "Oh. Oh. I did not know that." The enormity of her rudeness played on rewind in her mind. She knew her face turned an ugly splotchy pink, like a lobster with measles, when she was embarrassed. She took a step back, wondering if she'd look even more deranged if she turned around and ran away. "Well, that's very kind of you, and one can't complain about that type of customer service." When she brought herself to look at the man again, he smiled.

He held out his hand. "I'm Max Shepard." The man had soft dark eyes and short unruly hair.

"Sophie Berlin. Um, Ms. Berlin." Having a moment to inventory him, Max Shepard was very attractive with an outdoorsy, rugged aesthetic. *He looks like he stepped out of a calendar for lumberjacks.* "Well, Mr. Shepard, if you could have the tennis rackets there by tomorrow morning, that would be great. Good evening."

"Good evening, Sophie."

Sophie, though determined to stroll out of the store with dignity and seat herself gracefully into her car, slid on a patch of ice but regained her balance. She stole a quick glance back. *Of course he's watching.*

Way to keep it classy, Sophie. Now he thinks you have anger management issues AND you're uncoordinated. It's okay. It doesn't matter. You don't have time for a flirtation right now anyway.

Early the next morning, Sophie arrived at the tennis club. Their facility was not as posh as Foxcroft's Tarlington Pavilion, but it did have stands for spectators and a snack bar, so it suited the tournament's needs well.

Inside, Sophie met an excited group of kids. Ten- to fourteen-year-olds waved rackets, bounced balls, and a few late-comers were still lacing up their shoes. "Good morning. Everybody, Ms. Anna is going to help you warm up. Piper, I promised you I'd help you with your backhand."

A tall girl with glasses ran over. "Good morning, Ms. B." A young four-year-old girl trailed behind her. "Matty, you're not supposed to be on the court! Go back to Mom in the stands. I said go on!" The toddler looked stricken but obeyed. "Sorry about my little sister. I can't go anywhere without her. It's kind of a pain."

"It's okay. I'd have killed to have a sister growing up. I would've even settled for a brother." Sophie smiled and nudged Piper. "Now, let's get your killer backhand ready for the tournament."

Sophie began by demonstrating her backhand in slow motion and asked the girl to mimic her movements.

Piper concentrated, trying hard to do exactly as Sophie had done, then stopped. "What's on your handle, Ms. B?"

"This is grip tape. Tennis players apply extra tape to shape their grips to their personal style of holding the handle."

"Can I do that, too?"

"Of course you can." She jogged over to her duffle bag and pulled out her roll of black grip tape and handed it to her. "You keep it."

"I can have it? Thanks Ms. B.!"

"Well, I'm already sharing my epic backhand secrets, so why not? Let's get back to it."

After an hour of practice, Sophie gave the kids a snack break while her and Anna set up a few banners.

Sophie climbed a ladder while Anna held it steady.

"Hey, Sophie!" Mr. Muller, the owner of the tennis club, approached the girls.

"Be with you in a minute," Sophie yelled over her shoulder.

She climbed down, blowing her bangs out of her eyes.

"Sophie," said Muller, "I know you're busy, but I'd like to introduce you to the chair umpire and all-around judge I got for the tournament. He's great. Hot-shot tennis player back in the day. Really knows his stuff."

Sophie turned to see Mr. Muller standing with Max from Order of Play Sports.

Max wore a huge grin. "Good morning. Nice to see you again, Sophie."

"Oh, you two have met already?" asked Muller.

Sophie tidied her hair. "Yes, I met Mr. Shepard yesterday, as a matter of fact. I saw the tennis rackets were already here this morning. Thank you."

"My pleasure. I brought them over last night. Some customers get angry about delays." Max gave her a mischievous grin.

He's enjoying this, thought Sophie. *It's probably a bad idea to kick the tournament umpire in the shins.*

"Okay," said Muller, "I'll let you all get on with whatever this is," and lost no time scurrying away.

Sophie searched for something to say. "Um, I'll be over here." She started up the ladder again.

Max walked over to the umpire stand. "And I'll be up here. I want to check out my new digs."

Sophie climbed the ladder, wishing it led to an alternate universe. *I'll be over here? That was a stupid thing to say, Sophie. You're not some married couple shopping at Costco.*

Anna handed her another banner. "Why are you all splotchy? You're not coming down with something, are you?"

"Don't be silly."

"Who's the cute judge?"

"That's the guy from the sports store I told you about."

"The one from yesterday? The one you blasted between the eyes and then had to eat your words?"

"That's not *exactly* how events played out but . . . yes."

"He's really cute. And he watched your form when you cowered away, and I don't mean your tennis swing. Hey, you're getting all speckled again—ohhhh, you like him! You like the sexy judge!"

"Shut up. I do not. I don't have time for your nonsense. I've got work to do."

Later that day, Sophie noticed Anna and Max in conversation. She made an excuse to straighten a banner nearby.

Anna noticed her lurking about. "Sophie, your pal Max and I are talking coffee. Sophie's fiercely loyal to Brewster's Coffee. Stops there every single morning."

"They do have the best coffee in town," Sophie said.

"I'll let you two talk coffee. Taran's on her way. She wants to pitch in." Anna walked away.

Sophie watched her go. *Subtle, Anna, real subtle.*

"Sophie, I'd like to invite you out for coffee, or what do they say now? I'd like to invite you out for pumpkin spice macchiato?"

"That's actually my favorite drink." Sophie bit her lip. "I'm really busy with the tournament. . . ." She started to pick up a box of decorations and festive streamers.

He quickly bent down and picked up the box to hand to her. "What I meant to say was that since you grab a coffee every morning at around . . . What time?"

"Seven thirty," Sophie said, with reluctance.

"Then I might just happen to grab a coffee at the same time. No pressure involved. Just two adults consuming coffee beverages around the same time as millions of other Americans. Right?"

"Right."

"Great. I may run into you in the morning then."

The next morning, Sophie noticed Max's Land Rover in the parking lot as soon as she pulled into Brewster's Coffee Shop. A light sleeting rain was falling over the cold cloudy morning.

She checked her hair in the rear-view mirror, took a deep breath, then walked into the coffee shop with her best and breeziest 'this is no big deal' face on. The thick aroma of fresh-brewed coffee and warm cinnamon surrounded her, both comforting and familiar. Brewster's had a wall of windows on one side letting in lots of natural light, and the floor was dotted with dark industrial wood tables of exposed wood grain, giving it the perfect blend of modern and rustic character. The buzz of conversations filled the space with the occasional coffee order call-outs.

Max stood up when she came in. "Good morning, Sophie."

For God's sake, this guy even looks handsome at seven thirty in the morning. That's not even normal.

"How are you?"

"Definitely ready for coffee. I've just ordered your pumpkin spice macchiato. Since you love this place, can you recommend anything?"

"Uhm, the cardamom latte is pretty nice,"

Max smiled and turned to the counter. "Sir, I'll have the cardamom latte."

A young barista, who looked about fifteen years old, asked, "Would you like whole milk, skim milk, soy milk, oat milk, almond milk, or coconut milk?"

"Do you have yak's milk?" Max said.

"What? Uhm, I'll have to ask my manager."

"Never mind. The whole milk is fine."

"Okay, here's your pumpkin spice macchiato. We're a bit behind, so it might take a few minutes on the latte."

Max turned to Sophie and gestured to a table for two in the back. "I'm going to have to wait a minute on mine, so why don't we sit down? Just for a minute."

"I suppose it's the least I can do to thank you for my P.S.M."

Max pulled out a chair for her.

Is this guy for real? Sophie thought. *Manners and everything?*

She sat down then began laughing. "Yak's milk?"

"Honestly, I wasn't sure what to say. I didn't even know that many *kinds* of milk existed."

"Hardcore coffee drinkers must seem hopeless to the rest of the world."

"I hear you teach at Foxcroft Academy? Do you like it?"

"Do I like being game mistress at Hoity-Toity High? Honestly, and surprisingly, I do. I get to make a living from tennis. That's what I love."

"Why did you decide to have a tournament?"

"Well, when Anna told me about the funds needed for a new burn unit at Children's Hospital, I wanted to do something. But more than that, I feel like I'm in this privileged niche of coaching. I didn't grow up wealthy, but I got to participate in tennis and track. All kids should be able to participate in sports, even compete in sports if they work hard." Sophie put a packet of sugar in her macchiato and gave it a stir. "What about you? Why a sports store?"

"I was also a tennis kid growing up. And track, and soccer, and any other team I could get on. I'm an only child, so I loved being part of a team. I probably would've played tennis professionally, but I wasn't quite good enough. Turns out I like business as well, so, in the end, I guess it worked out."

A barista called out, "Max, your cardamom latte is ready!"

Max got up to retrieve his order. "Never thought I'd hear those words. Excuse me a sec, Sophie."

What are you doing, Sophie? Snap out of it. What're you, thirteen?

Sophie jumped up and met Max coming back to the table. "Well, this was fun, but I guess I better get to the tennis club. I'm meant to be working."

"Okay. Hey, the sleet's turning to snow. I've got an umbrella. I'll walk you to your car."

On the quick walk, Max held the umbrella over Sophie, not himself.

She drove away biting her lip. "This might be a problem."

At the tennis club, Piper trailed behind Sophie all morning and searched for any opportunity to help her. Ironically, her little sister Matty did the same to her.

Piper was outraged. "If you don't stop, I'm telling Mom!"

"No!" Matty yelled.

Sophie thought it was time to step in. "Piper, it's okay." She bent down to Matty. "Matty, would you like to help?"

The four-year-old's excited miniature body reminded Sophie of a bobblehead toy.

"Good. I need someone to pick up balls and put them in the baskets. Can you do that for me?"

The little girl's face lit up like a firefly, and she ran off and began carefully picking up the balls strewn all over the court. One by one, she took the tennis balls and threw them into the large metal baskets, each time making the noise "Boooop" when they hit the bottom.

Sophie laughed out loud. "Good job, Matty! I love the sound effects."

She turned to go back to coaching Piper but noticed Max leaning against the wall watching her. Feeling suddenly self-conscious, she called to the kids, "All right, kids, gather 'round. Ms. Anna's going to take you through warmups now."

She sneaked a peek a few more times and found Max still watching with his mischievous smile.

A few mornings later, Sophie was dashing into Brewster's for her morning coffee and found Max in line. *Yikes! I haven't even had a chance to fix my hair yet.*

"Good morning, Max. Here again?"

"Good morning. Well, once you've experienced a cardamom latte, you can't see yourself returning to a spice-free wasteland. I'm glad I ran into you. Got time to sit for a minute? I had an idea about the tournament I wanted to run by you."

"All right."

Most of the tables were occupied in the busy café so they settled down in two side-by-side overstuffed chairs and shared a side table for their drinks. Indie folk music playing in the background was occasionally drowned out by the whirr of frothing dairy.

Sophie took a deep breath and sighed happily. "Why is the smell of coffee so intoxicating?"

Max looked hard at her. "It is intoxicating. Uhm, anyway. I've noticed Anna's been helping you warm up the kids before practice, and while Anna seems like a lovely, great person . . ."

"She's a terrible tennis player? Yeah, I know, but the kids love her and she works for free, so."

"I was just thinking since I'm around a lot anyway, maybe I could warm the kids up and that would give you more time to focus on individual players. Of course, I'm nowhere near as good as you, but—"

"That would actually be amazing. It's always a challenge for coaches to feel like you've given each child enough dedicated attention. And that would free me up to do that so, yes. I'll definitely take you up on that, if you're sure you'll have the time?"

"I'm sure. Good, that's settled. I had another idea. A buddy of mine is a reporter on the local paper. I thought if he did an article on the tournament, it would get the word out more about it and the need at Children's Hospital. But only if it'd be something you're interested in?"

"Yes, that'd be great. I sent all the press release stuff to the local papers, but a full article would really help."

"And it's the kind of local interest feel-good story the paper likes so he'd love to talk to you. Maybe even feature a few of the kids." He passed a business card to Sophie. "Here's his info."

She felt an electric sensation when his hand brushed her fingers. "This will really help, Max. I appreciate you suggesting it. The kids will be so excited."

They continued to talk for another half hour about warm-up strategies before they left.

The next day, Max took the kids through their warm-ups while Sophie worked one-on-one with a twelve-year-old named Michael. His skills were far behind the other kids, but Sophie, determined to give him a shot in the tournament, went over the basic etiquette again for positioning and movement during a match.

"It's a lot of fussy rules, I know, but you'll get it. And I'm always here if you forget or have questions."

He smiled but wouldn't meet Sophie's eye.

After warming up and practicing about an hour, the kids went off with Anna for snacks.

Max helped Sophie pick up the balls in metal baskets. "Hey, I hope Anna's okay with me taking over."

"Are you kidding? She's thrilled! Now she can just hang out with the kids."

When Max had picked up the last ball, he said, "You want to hit the ball with me back and forth a little, just for fun?"

"Okay. If you think you'll survive the experience."

"Ohhhh and the trash talking starts immediately! Okay."

"Two short sets? That should get us through meal break." She positioned herself behind the baseline and blew her bangs out of her eyes. "And just to give you a fair chance, you serve first."

He nodded and bounced the ball a few times, then flung it in the air and sent it angled with sidespin right of the center mark.

"Nice," Sophie said, aggressively returning his serve. *This guy's pretty good. But let's see how good.*

Play continued back and forth, neither holding back, return after return. A few of the kids and adults couldn't resist wandering over to watch the action. Sophie's backhand was relentless, and she moved deftly across the court like a prize fighter, never resting her feet in one position. Her focus absolute, everything and everyone outside the court fell away, and there was only the reverberating constant rhythmic whack of the tennis ball.

Ten minutes in, Max, sweaty and out of breath, showed signs of fatigue. It was Sophie's serve, and she shot a slice to the edge of the deuce side, drawing Max out. He just managed to meet the serve and return, and Sophie took the advantage and returned to the far opposite side. Max dove for it, falling to the ground just as the ball bounced.

Sophie sprinted over and offered him a hand up. "That's 4-0, I'm afraid."

Max gulped air, trying to recover. "Yes. Four-love. Well played. You're crazy good, you know," he said, holding on to her hand.

"Thanks." She bit her lip, exhilarated by his closeness.

"I think I underestimated how rusty I am."

"You weren't too bad. You surprised me. You're actually pretty fast."

"You're faster. You're very talented." Max stared into her eyes.

The intensity suddenly made her feel self-conscious. She pulled away. "Well, I'm going to see if the kids are finished with their snack." Sophie walked away but couldn't resist looking back. He was watching.

She walked over to Anna and the kids. Anna whispered, "Did you really have to annihilate the sexy judge?"

"He held his own okay."

"I guess, and he didn't even throw a tantrum when he lost. I'm just saying. In case it isn't obvious, I'm Team Max."

"Calm down, Tiger. Let's just get through the tournament."

For the next few days, Sophie kept running into Max at Brewster's and somehow, wrapped in the glow of milk froth, cardamom, and easy jazz played over the loudspeaker, they kept sitting down for conversations. It often began with tournament to-do lists then slowly developed into deeper talks.

"I guess I've achieved a lot of my professional goals," Max said. They were perched at a high-top table with their coffee, Sophie's duffle was slung over the back of her chair.

Max had a blueberry muffin and, after cutting it in half, offered it to her.

Sophie took it. "Thanks, didn't have time for breakfast this morning."

"Here, let me get you a napkin." He came back to the table with napkins and a few extra packets of sugar. "Where was I?"

"Professional goals."

"Oh yeah. My business is successful, most of the time. I like the independence. I like meeting new people. I'm where I want to be. What're your long-term goals, Sophie? I've seen you with the kids. They really love you."

This made her smile. "They're great kids. I suppose the ultimate dream would be to start my own tennis camp. To start seasonally, and the rest of the year I could teach private lessons. I truly enjoy working with the kids."

"I can tell. I've watched you while you're coaching. You had this smile about you. I think you were dream-basking a little."

"That's a good way to put it." She smiled. *Who is this guy?*

"I can tell this tournament means a lot to you." Max took a long sip of his coffee, smelling the deep roast. "Okay, so that's professional goals. What about personal goals?"

She rolled her eyes. "C'mon. Do you have personal goals?"

"Of course, I bought an old Craftsman house last year and I'm restoring it. It's the one on the corner of Bay Street."

Sophie sat up straight in her chair. "That's you? That place looks great! It's funny, here I was imagining an old happy retired couple living there."

"I hope someday that'll be true."

We're just friends. You can always use more friends.

After a moment of quiet, Max asked, "What're you thinking about?"

Sophie said, "I'm just thinking I better get a refill for the road."

Later that day, she'd arranged for the reporter, Andrew, to stop by the tennis club. At drop off that morning, she'd informed all the parents he was coming and may be taking pictures of their practice.

After the interview, Max approached them and shook hands with Andrew. "Is this old hack treating your right, Sophie?"

"Yes, he's been great. The kids loved the attention."

Andrew pointed at Sophie. "And did the camera love this one. She's a dream subject. Human interest with a good-looking exterior. The article will sell itself. And I better get on it if I want it to print in the morning's paper. Thanks again, Sophie. Best of luck." He shook hands with her and was off.

"I'm glad you suggested that Max."

"Andrew will be a good contact for the future when you're ready to start your tennis camp."

Sophie smiled. "Good idea."

Max tapped his temple then pointed to his feet. "Up here for thinking, down there for dancing. Do you like to dance, Sophie?"

"Only on the court," she said and twirled off back to practice.

The next morning over pumpkin spice macchiatos, Max and Sophie sat at the good table by the row of windows. The freezing temperatures and threat of snow had kept a lot of people indoors and out of coffeehouses, but all the familiar smells hung in the air: roasted coffee, cinnamon, and steaming milk. They even had a mulled cider, which Max ordered.

"How's the cider?"

"It's good actually. It makes me feel very Dickensian, but I'd still rather have a good old-fashioned cup of coffee."

"Right? Okay, the music they're piping in is killing me a little bit."

"I hadn't even noticed it."

"It's that coffeehouse background indie/folk/soul that could be on a playlist entitled *Guys Having Feelings*."

Max laughed. "I hear it happens to the best of us."

"Believe it when I see it."

"C'mon. You're kidding?"

"I am, sort of. But seriously, young men even call it 'catching feelings' now like they're talking about malaria."

"You're really funny, Sophie. Those are young, immature guys. They'll learn."

"Learn what?" She leaned in.

"That if you're lucky enough to have the right woman by your side, she'll make you more of a man, not less of one."

I feel like this is a Dickensian conversation. Am I talking to Mr. Darcy? His hair has the cutest curls at the back—stop it, Sophie! Friend zone!

"I think I'm going to get my prescribed cardamom latte. Be right back." Max rose and went to the counter while Sophie checked her phone. She sent a few texts about the tournament until he came back.

Max came up behind Sophie's chair and put a hand on her shoulder. "Look what I found for sale at the counter." Max laid a CD down on the table. "It's a gift. I thought you might not have *Dudes with Feelings* in your collection. The warmth of his hand sent a tingle down her spine.

She feigned concern. "Thanks a lot. But I think it's sad that actual men had to be hurt during the making of this album."

"How do you think they managed to get a feeling out of them?"

"With men, there's only one foolproof way: pulling nose hairs."

"Funny and graphic." Max sat back down and took a good look at her. "So, I want to know more about your tennis journey. Did you ever play professionally?"

"I did, for a while. I did well, but eventually had to find a grown-up job."

"Are you an only child like me? Is that why you think you fell in love with tennis?"

"I am an only child, but that wasn't the reason." She began flipping the CD over and over in her hands.

"What was the reason?"

"I guess the tennis court was like this island where rules were defined, matches had order, and anything out of bounds didn't go unchecked. It wasn't like that at home." Sophie looked deep into her drink. "Maybe I've never found another space that made sense to me as much as a tennis court does. I guess that's why I like teaching and coaching. I'm giving some of that safe feeling to another kid. Tennis is the love of my life."

"Your life's not over yet, Sophie."

Sophie felt her stomach somersault like the euphoric motion of an amusement park ride.

"Well, the tournament starts tomorrow. Excited?" Max asked.

"Yes, but I've still got plenty on my to-do list."

"Oh, you're one of those?"

"Those?"

"The list-making tribe. I knew it the moment I met you."

"The moment you met me. You mean when I stormed into your store and yelled at you like a reject from an anger management class?"

He gave her his mischievous grin again. "I thought it was kind of hot."

Sophie bit her lip. *God, I would love to kiss this man right now.*

A young woman sashayed up to the table. "Max? Max, honey, is that you? It's *so* good to see you."

Max looks surprised. "Katrina? When did you get back in town?"

Katrina gave Max a big hug. "About a week ago. My family's been begging me to move back. How've you been? You look great. How're your parents?"

"Um, fine. Excuse me, Katrina, this is Sophie. She's in charge of the big charity tournament that's going on right now."

"You and your sports, Max. Nice to meet you, Sophia."

"Sophie. My pleasure."

Who's the Brazilian supermodel? Maybe he's more into looks than I thought. Is this an old girlfriend or someone who's still semi in the picture?

Katrina grabbed Max's phone off the table. "Here, I'm going to put my new number in for you. Call me. Let's get together now that I'm living in East Aurora again. Okay? Gotta run."

The young woman jetted out the door like a power-walker.

Max sat back down and started to pick up his coffee cup but fumbled it, the molten hot brew spilling all over the table and dousing his phone. He grabbed it quickly, burning his finger. "Damnit!" he yelled, grasping for napkins.

Sophie startled. *I've never heard Max raise his voice before.* She checked her phone, not wanting to look at him. "Speaking of running. You know I really should be getting to the tennis club. To-do lists." She jumped up, slinging her duffle over her shoulder, and rushing for the door.

Max got up, too. "Hey, Sophie! I'm sorry. Slow down. Wait a minute—"

But Sophie didn't stop until she'd made it to her car. She sped off feeling like she might cry, and she couldn't even explain why.

Why did that bother you so much? You and Max are just friends. Don't be stupid here, Sophie. A guy that good looking is probably keeping his options open. Don't set yourself up for a heartbreak here. Think about your career. That's what's important. At any rate, this nonsense can wait until after the tournament.

The first morning of the tournament, Sophie woke up early, made coffee at home, and drank it with Constance purring comfortably in her lap. She drove past Brewster's and didn't look in the rear-view mirror.

When she got to the tennis club, Anna opened the door for her. "Good morning. Any last-minute to-do lists that Taran and I can help you with?"

"Thanks. Where is Taran?"

Anna pointed to the concession stand, where Taran appeared to be in a serious talk with the attendant. "She's in a complicated doctrinal conversation with that guy about the correct batter consistency for corndogs. Where's Max?"

"I'm sure he'll be along."

"You didn't have coffee with him this morning?"

"I didn't have time today. Can you make sure there's plenty of water for the kids?"

"Sophie? This is me here. I know you. Something happened. I thought it was going so well. Max was such a nice surprise that just happened to come along with this tournament."

Sophie blew her bangs out of her eyes. "It's better to stop now before the bad surprises."

"Soph."

"Oh, some of my kids are here already. I think we're going to have a good crowd."

Sensing she should drop the subject, Anna took a moment to look around the large festive pavilion. "Sophie, you've done an amazing job here, really. I'm proud of you, sis." Anna gave her a big hug.

"It is pretty great, isn't it?" she said, elation washing over her.

"Can you believe it? This place is packed to the rafters. I guess that piece in the local paper really did the trick."

"Yes, I'm grateful for that. And I couldn't have done this tournament without your help. Thank you. I'm sure I haven't said that enough." Sophie looked around trying to absorb everything, remember everything. *All the late nights, the details, the patience—it was worth it.* "Dream-basking," she whispered.

Anna looked puzzled. "What?"

"Never mind. With what's left from sponsors and ticket sales, we've raised close to $10,000 already. Mr. Muller is also going to add the profit from concession sales!"

"Wow! You did all this, Sophie! The hospital board is going to be blown away."

"Okay, okay, enough celebrating. Let's get these kids ready to play." Sophie began some warm up drills with the kids while Anna took the opportunity to snap a few pictures of Sophie with the children. The kids were vibrating with nervous energy, and several times she had to redirect their eyes off the crowd milling in. "Michael, Grayson, your match will be first."

"Me?" squeaked Michael.

"Yes, you. I have something for you." She reached into her pocket and pulled out a small medallion. "This is for my most-improved player, and remember, no matter what happens in this match, you've come the furthest of anyone."

The boy held the medallion in his palm. He beamed with pride. The other kids clapped and gathered around to congratulate him. Michael let them all have a turn seeing his medallion.

Soon the tennis club was full to capacity with lots of chatter and movement, a small line at the snack bar, and a packed set of stands. Proud parents pointed to their children with one hand and waved hot-dogs or parcels of popcorn wildly around with the other. Occasional camera flashes burst from the crowd.

Sophie saw Max and Mr. Muller step onto the court. Max smiled and waved to her. She nodded, then looked away. *Please not now. My head needs to be in the game for the kids.*

He jogged over. "I didn't see you at Brewster's this morning. Just wanted to say good luck." He squeezed her arm and headed for the umpire stand.

She tried to shake off the goosebumps induced from the warm touch of his hand. Once play began, Sophie had laser-focus on the game. Michael and Grayson both played well, Grayson just managing to win the match. Michael jogged over to shake his hand.

Max made eye contact with Sophie, but she looked away again.

Next, Piper, Sophie's strongest player, prepared for her match. Sophie was giving her a last-minute pep talk when Matty ran up and took Piper's racket.

"Matty, give it back!" she shrieked.

"I wanna play," said Matty.

Matty's mom ran onto the court and picked her up. "Stop sneaking away. Now give your sister her racket back and wish her luck."

Matty returned the tennis racket and said quietly, "Luck." Then she buried her face in her mom's shirt.

After they went back into the stands, Max, amused by the scene, called out, "Coach? Are your players ready for the next match?"

She nodded.

Sophie had paired Piper with Marissa. Marissa wasn't as far along as Piper—she didn't have another player as strong as her—but Sophie thought Marissa, as the oldest, the most capable of holding her own compared to the other kids.

Piper played well and strategically, just like Sophie had taught her. *She'll be as good as me someday if she works hard.*

Sophie shook her head, trying to clear her thoughts. *Okay, I know you're proud of Piper, but watch favoring her, Sophie. It's not fair to the others.*

After around forty-five minutes of play, Max announced the score: "Game, Piper Landry, 40-15."

Piper held up her hands and pranced around the court.

A little too much ego there. We've got to work on that, Sophie thought as she went out to meet her. "Piper, stop shaking your booty and go shake Marissa's hand. Congratulate her. It was a good game."

Piper, immediately obedient, jogged over and shook Marissa's hand, then hugged her. Sophie gave her a thumbs-up of approval.

The loudspeaker clicked on again. "We will now have a short intermission. Play will resume in thirty minutes."

Chaos overtook the tennis pavilion as everyone left the stands and the noise level rose. Sophie decided to check with concessions and make sure they had plenty of provisions for the rest of the day. On her way, she literally ran into Max, and they almost bumped heads.

Max said, "Hey, I've been hoping to catch up with you all morning. Look, I know you're busy, but I just want to be clear. I did date Katrina—two years ago. Then she moved away. Until yesterday, I literally hadn't seen her in those two years."

"We're not married, so there's no reason you have to explain that to me."

"Okay, but I'm sensing some weird energy from you. I just want you to know it was a casual dating relationship that I have no interest in renewing."

Sophie sighed. "She seemed to know your parents. That doesn't sound casual. Just be honest with me."

"I've always been honest with you, Sophie. Yeah, Katrina met my parents because she showed up at the store one day when my parents happened to be there."

"Okay, listen, this is not about some stupid ex-girlfriend who can't pronounce my name."

"Are you sure? Because it feels like it is. Or like maybe it's about something else I don't really get right now. For two weeks we've been talking over coffee, getting to know each other, and I guess I couldn't help but hope this might be going somewhere—"

A loud *bang* startled them.

A primal fear jolted through Sophie, overwhelming her, immediately signaling that something had gone seriously wrong.

"What happened!?! What is it?" Sophie asked Max.

"I don't know," he said, looking around wildly.

The crowd had turned to utter chaos. Everyone crowded around the umpire stand. Sophie broke through the crowd. A little girl lay on the floor, wailing.

"Matty! It's Matty!" Sophie dropped to the floor next to her. "Are you hurt, Matty?!"

Anna ran over. "She fell. I guess she climbed up the umpire stand to have a look around at the crowd and fell off. It was so busy and crowded, no one saw her head up there."

Sophie tried to hug Matty, but the child kept flailing and sobbing. "What should we do, Anna?"

"I think she's definitely hurt."

Max pushed through the crowd. "Is there something I can do?"

Anna stood. "Max, call 911. She should definitely be seen in the ER. They'll be able to do imaging. It's better if we let them move her."

Matty's mom and her sister, Piper, rode with Matty in the ambulance. As it pulled away, Anna hugged Sophie.

"Oh, Anna, this is the worst thing that could've happened," Sophie said. "I'll, uh . . . I'll go back inside and send everyone home and announce the tournament will carry on tomorrow as scheduled. I need to get to the hospital."

An hour later, Sophie, Anna, and Max sat in the ER waiting room. It was cold inside the large, impersonal space with the automatic doors opening constantly and admitting frigid gusts of wind from outside. Rows of hard, plastic chairs lined the walls and foul odors fought against strong disinfectant.

Sophie stood and paced back and forth.

Anna also got up. "Let me see if I can go find something out."

"Thanks." Sophie sat back down.

"Is this my fault? Did I distract you?" Max said.

"No. I'm the adult in charge, so it falls on me. I can't sit still. I'm going upstairs for some coffee." Sophie wanted to cry, and she didn't want to do it in front of Max.

In the elevator she let the tears come. *This is why I don't date, why I keep my focus. So I don't let bad things happen.*

The fresh coffee gave her some stability, and she had pulled herself together by the time she got off the elevator and back to the ER. But as she walked down the hallway toward the waiting room, just before she turned the corner, she heard Max and Anna's speaking, and something in their tone made her stop instinctively and listen.

Max was saying, "I feel like she's retreating back in her shell."

"Well, she probably is. Look, beautiful women often attract guys that are just interested in their looks. Guys that aren't serious—aren't serious about her or much of anything else. And most importantly, are unsupportive. I've known her since college, and Sophie's had a lot of that. She's had a lot of guys that let her down. Of course she's going to be skeptical."

"Yeah, I admit she's the most beautiful woman I've ever seen, but ... she's also funny and smart in a unique way. Sophie's got this intense drive. On the court, she's a machine, but then she can be so gentle with the kids. She challenges them to be better, and they do it because they want to please her. She's beautiful in a million quiet, surprising ways. It's like this exquisite mystery I just want to keep unraveling. I can't believe I found somebody like her. I only want her to let me in a little."

"Be patient. I know she has a monster of a wall up, but believe me, it's worth getting to the other side."

"Anna, I wouldn't have met her for coffee again and again, I wouldn't have been hanging around the tennis club all this time, if I didn't really want to get to know her. I don't even know what the hell cardamom is. I just want a chance. . . .

"Yesterday, I run into an old girlfriend I would've never thought of reconnecting with, and it kind of threw me off guard, then spilled my coffee and ruined my phone, so I guess I was a little mad, but she just ran out of there before I could stop her."

"Oh, I see. This is what you need to understand about Sophie: her mother is practically a saint, but her father can be volatile: throwing tantrums, kicking doors open, breaking stuff to make a point."

"Are we talking abusive?"

"Oh no, he never hit anybody, just controlled everybody with his anger. I can never understand why her mother stayed with him. She just goes on adoring him no matter what he does. They met in college, both studying to become architects. They got married after graduation and her father insisted her mother give up her career. So, Sophie grew up thinking love was this unsafe, sometimes even frightening thing where her mom just got swallowed up."

Sophie felt flush with anger then embarrassment.

Anna kept going: "Maybe I shouldn't have told you all this, and I'll have to let her know that I did, but I think you could be good for her. Sophie deserves to be happy. She's far too special to be alone."

"Thank you for telling me."

"Don't thank me. If you hurt Sophie, I'll sweep your legs and shave your head. I'm serious."

"Fair enough."

Sophie took a few deep breaths, then walked into the waiting room. "Did you find out anything?"

Anna started. "Y-Yes." She cleared her throat and stole a quick—guilty, Sophie thought—glance at Max. "I talked to Matty's mother. Matty's been seen by a doctor and he sent her for X-rays, but he's thinking it's only a broken arm."

Sophie suddenly felt ashamed of her anger and embarrassment. The thought of a little girl in a big hospital bed put everything in perspective. Nothing could matter less than her love life or wounded ego at this moment. She sat back down. They waited two more hours.

With great relief, they finally saw Matty, a cast on her arm, being wheeled out in a wheelchair by her mom with Piper trailing close behind.

Matty smiled when she saw them.

"Look what I got, Ms. B! Mom says people can write their names on it or draw dogs and flowers and I don't even have to wash it anymore."

Sophie knelt next to her. "Does it hurt?"

"It did, but it's better. Will you write your name on it?"

"You want *me* to?" Sophie looked up at Matty's mom. "It happened on my watch. It's a coach's worst nightmare. That a kid gets hurt."

Matty's mom smiled. "I should've been watching her."

Piper said, "Me too." She looked sheepish and clung to her mother's hand. A big contrast to the braggadocious Piper who had won the match.

"I should've been watching, too. I'm sorry," Sophie said.

Matty's mom put her arm around Piper. "I know. But it's all been a great adventure to Matty. She'll be fine. They both still want to be just like you when they grow up."

Sophie sighed. Anna handed her a pen. Sophie signed her name on the cast and wrote *I heart you*, then gave her a big hug.

Max walked Anna and Sophie to their car.

"Hey, thanks for staying, Max," Anna said.

"I wasn't going anywhere."

Sophie looked up then and met his eyes. *Am I really ready to walk away from this man?*

On the drive home, Sophie sat still and quiet while Anna drove. When they pulled into their apartment complex, Anna stopped the car. "You okay, Soph?"

"I don't know. Tonight was a lot. Another big day tomorrow." Sophie started to open her car door. The handle was cold, and the window glass coated with frost.

"Wait," Anna said. She took a deep breath. "We need to talk. I had a conversation with Max tonight. I told him a little about your parents—"

"I know. I heard you." Sophie leaned her head against the chilly glass. The sky was almost black and too cold for stars.

"I'm sorry, Sophie. I guess it wasn't really my story to tell. I'm just worried you're going to miss out on a full life, on things you really deserve. But still, if I'm out of line, I apologize." Anna grabbed Sophie's hand and held it. "I mean it, Soph."

"It's okay. I guess things got complicated, huh?" Her heart ached. She felt vulnerable and small.

"I just want to help but, of course, it goes without saying that whatever you decide about Max is your decision. I'll support you either way."

Sophie hugged her for a few moments. "It does go without saying, but thank you for saying it."

"Are we good?"

"Good."

Anna took her hand again and gave it a little squeeze. "What are you going to do about Max?"

Match

THE LAST DAY OF THE tournament fell four days before Christmas. Sophie hosted a small ceremony at the end and awarded medals to the top-ranking winners.

"Now I want all the kids who played in the tournament to come to the stage. C'mon, all of you."

A loud shuffling, uncoordinated group of kids made their way to the stage. Sophie waited patiently until all of them stood around her, and then she peered through the crowd until she saw Matty sitting on her mother's lap. Sophie crooked a finger, motioning for the little girl to come to the stage. Matty's mom helped her down, and she ran to her sister.

"Thanks to all of you kids. You worked hard and you're all my champs. Because of you, we can help lots of sick children. I also want to thank all the sponsors. You'll notice their banners hanging around. And also, thank you to Mr. Muller for graciously hosting us."

The crowd applauded and Sophie waited for it to die down a bit. "Lastly, I want to ask the members of the Children's Hospital Board to come up, please." Once they were all standing behind her, she held up a check. "On behalf of everyone who worked so hard to make this three-day event happen, I am thrilled to present you with a check for $18,000 toward the new burn unit for Children's Hospital."

As the crowd cheered, Sophie looked around for Max and saw him to the left of the stage. She smiled all the things she wished she could say to him and, in a crazy way, she felt like he heard her.

When the festivities were over, there remained nothing left to do but clean up. Two hours later, an exhausted Sophie found Anna in the stands checking her text messages. "Well, it's all finished. I'm not sure what to do with myself now."

"Now enjoy the holidays. Eat too much. Drink too much. Nap in between."

"I'm leaving tomorrow for my mother's."

"I didn't think you were spending more than one night there."

"I wasn't. Mom called last night. My dad was upset I was only spending one night at home."

"So, your mom, queen of the codependent relationship, called you to ask you to stay a few more nights?"

"Apparently his meltdowns warm her heart. Besides, it wouldn't be Christmas without a pregame beer-fueled rant from my dad."

"So, you staying a few extra nights is finally going to make your dad happy, is it?"

"Dad's 'happy' is an oscillating scale between miserable and vindicated. But I do miss my mom, so it'll be fine."

"I'm sorry, Sophie."

"It's okay. What are you and Taran doing for Christmas?"

"Well, since we'll be cat sitting—"

"Thank you both."

"We are doing Chinese food and binge-watching travel shows." She showed Sophie a watchlist on her phone.

"Sounds like heaven."

"It's heaven because I won't be alone."

"I won't be alone." She got up and started walking.

Anna followed. "You'll be with your parents. I'm afraid you'll feel alone. You know, Sophie, now that the tournament's over, you won't have any reason to see Max anymore."

"Oh, yes, I guess that's right."

"Okay, it's a mistake to let that man get away, and that's a lesbian saying it. I'm serious, I think he's a really good guy. Who knows when another that genuine will come along again."

"I don't know. Max confuses me, distracts me. Maybe it's for the best."

"For the best how? Sex is supposed to distract you, Sophie! Love is the distraction that reminds us we're supposed to be living a full life, not just hiding in a few safe compartments. Look, Max hung around half the night with you in the ER. He's practically been doing backflips to get your attention. He's been putting himself out there for weeks, Sophie. I know you haven't meant to, but you've kind of been testing him for faults and he proved himself. He didn't go anywhere. *And* I think he's still in the parking lot. I'm just saying."

"I'll think about it." She felt her phone vibrating. Sophie pulled it from her back pocket and twirled it round. "It's a text from my mom: 'Sorry we couldn't make it up for the tournament, but your dad's had too much going on for a car trip right now. I can't wait to hear all the news. I'm so happy you're coming home, Sophie bug!'" She sighed and dropped her arms. "Oh, Anna, maybe it was a mistake to agree to three days at home. I mean, I'm dying to see my mother, but I just wish . . ."

"You wish what?"

Sophie's mind flashed an image of her curled up in front of a cozy fire with Max. She flushed.

Anna smirked. "You're looking all splotchy again. Thinking about a hot holiday? Better go to the parking lot to cool off. Tick tock, Soph."

Sophie shook her head, but she was smiling. She picked up some papers. "I need to take this paperwork to Mr. Muller." Sophie walked to his office and found him talking to his wife.

"Thank you again, for everything. Have you seen Max?"

Mrs. Muller, a pleasant older woman with glasses and short curly hair, rushed over to give her a hug. "We were just talking to him outside. Yes, you should go give him a big thank-you for sponsoring the event."

Mr. Muller said, "Shhh, honey, that was a secret."

Sophie stopped. "Wait a minute, was Max the anonymous sponsor?"

Mr. Muller shrugged. "Yes, Max and Order of Play Sports, but he wanted to be anonymous. But my wife is always letting the cat out of the bag. But yes, he was very generous."

"Thank you for telling me. Max never said anything."

Mrs. Muller put her hands on her hips. "Well, he wouldn't. He's not that sort. That man is always helping in the community. Why, two years ago, when my husband had heart surgery, Max coordinated volunteers to help keep this place open. He never asks for thanks because he does everything for the right reasons, is what I say."

Sophie's mind whirled. "I guess it's a stark difference from the other sponsors who plastered their banners all over the place. Of course, it's their right to. I appreciate what they did to help Children's Hospital."

"Yes, and that's good but I'm just saying you don't see a man like Max Shepard prancing around a stage. He'd rather see the kids get the spotlight." She eyed Sophie intently and started nodding her head. "That man deserves a good woman, and a smart woman would snap him up, is what I say."

Sophie bit her lip so she wouldn't laugh. "Well, thank you both again for everything. Good night."

She retreated quickly from the office. *Geez! Are the matchmakers of the world teaming up against me? Must be the holiday spirit is turning everyone mushy. Still, it's kind of sweet.*

She hugged herself and leaned against the wall. *I can't believe Max was the anonymous sponsor and he never said anything. I suppose it wouldn't hurt to just wish him a Merry Christmas before he leaves.*

Sophie walked outside to find the parking lot empty.

"Merry Christmas, Max," she whispered as the dark sky began to spit a light snow.

When Sophie arrived at her parents' house, a blue two-story colonial, her mother came out to meet her with a big hug. "I'm so glad you're home, my Sophie bug. Come inside and get warm. I'll make a fire. Are you hungry?"

"Sure."

After the kitchen was filled with the smell of sautéed ham, onion, and peppers, they sat by the fireplace in the den together while Sophie ate her warm, creamy omelet. The taste made her feel like that ten-year-old again with Saturday morning omelets and cartoons.

"Is it good, Sophie bug?"

"Yummy, as always."

"Go say hello to your father. He's puttering in the garage. Stays there for hours."

"Okay." She brushed her bangs away from her eyes and straightened her blouse.

Sophie's dad sat huddled at a wooden workbench with a disheveled mix of tools scattered around. Behind him sat a display of miniature sailing vessel replicas. He was slightly balding now, and Sophie was startled by how small, how old, her father looked.

"Hi, Dad."

"Hi, Sophie. Drive okay?"

"Great. Smooth sailing." Sophie wondered why their conversations always consisted of a series of incomplete sentences.

"What way'd you take?"

"The 340."

"Not the best way. A6 would've saved you a good half hour."

"I'll remember on the way back." She wandered around the workshop looking at the perfection of each schooner, each sloop. The accuracy, the artistry always impressed her. "Well, Mom's made a pecan pie. I'm popping back in for a slice. Want one?"

"No. She made it too sweet for me. She knows I don't like it like that."

She took a deep breath. "Right."

Sophie got back to the kitchen to find a slice of pie cut and waiting. It was filled with a caramelly center and topped with candied, crunchy pecans and had just a warming finish of rum. Billie Holiday played in the background.

"Really delicious, Mom."

Sophie's mom hugged her. "Thanks for coming home. I know you're busy. Now you sent me a few pictures but tell me all about the tournament. It's so exciting, just like when you used to compete."

They talked for about an hour, then Sophie's mom looked pained. "Sophie, I want you to know how proud I am of you. You need to know that."

"I know, Mom. I know." She put her arm around her mom. "What is it? Is something wrong? Is it Dad?"

"Your father . . . there's good in your father. He just needs control to feel safe. Because he can't ever really trust the other person. Do you see? It's sad when you think about it. All these years I've lived my life for him, but he still can't just trust that I love him. I guess I wasn't the best role model for you. Sometimes in life we say we don't have a choice, but that's not always true. We just don't have a choice that wouldn't hurt other people. I probably should've protected you more." Sophie's mom wiped her eyes.

"Mom, it's okay. Really."

"But that's why I'm so proud of you. You're strong, and when you fall in love, it will be on your terms. I know you probably think I made the wrong choice when I chose your father and a family instead of a career."

"Are you ever sorry? Do you ever wonder what you missed?"

Her mother thought for a minute then smiled. "Sometimes. I think that's natural, but Sophie bug, I did make that choice. Yes, your father insisted, but I had the choice to walk away. Instead of designing buildings, I built a family, I built a beautiful Sophie. I think, somehow, you've got it in your head it *has to be* one or other, that there's only room for one because it was that way for me, but Sophie, you're wrong, you're a different person. You don't have to choose. You can have all those bright things in your head and a man in your heart, if that's what you want."

"How will I know? How will I really know it's a man I can trust?"

"You'll know you've found the right one when you find a man who loves you and who's strong enough to support your dreams because that's what *you* need."

Sophie suddenly felt glad she came.

Her father came into the kitchen. "Margaret, where did you put my chisel saw? You've moved the damn thing again! You know I can't finish my work without it."

"I'll come help you find it, Nathan." Her mother patted her hand as she scurried out of the kitchen.

After a huge Christmas Day dinner, Sophie felt stir-crazy and restless. Unable to sleep the night before, she knew the source of her misery but didn't dare give voice to it, even in her own head. Even though it was Christmas night, she decided to drive home. She kissed her mom goodbye and promised to come again New Year's Day. Her dad watched from the window. She smiled and waved.

The night was clear and biting cold. Sophie drove the two hours back to East Aurora without music, just the mornings she'd spent with Max replaying in her head—his eyes, his messy hair, his voice. She remembered the smell of his soap, like sandalwood on the beach. Her head ached with it.

Her mother's words repeated, "You'll know you've found the right one when you find a man who loves you and who's strong enough to support your dreams."

Sophie could suddenly see something so clearly that she'd somehow missed. She remembered Max driving two cities away to make sure the tennis rackets were available for the tournament, volunteering to warm up the kids before practice each day, serving as the tournament umpire, staying with her at the hospital until they found out Matty was okay, setting up a news article to help promote the tournament, and she'd just discovered he was a generous anonymous sponsor before they'd even met.

She realized her tournament, her big success, wouldn't have been the success it was if Max weren't in the picture, and if he hadn't continued to actively support her dream after they'd gotten to know each other. *And I don't think I ever even said thank you. Not once. Is it too late to fix it?*

She drove straight to Max's house on Bay Street. Sophie sighed with relief. The lights were on, the Christmas tree still lit. She made it to the front door but couldn't bring herself to knock.

What if he doesn't want to see me? What if he's had time to think about it and he's decided he doesn't want me?

Sophie retreated from the porch but only made it halfway to the driveway when the door opened and Max stepped onto the porch to get firewood. "Sophie? Hey, Sophie."

She turned and walked back to the porch but didn't ascend the stairs.

"I-I realized that I hadn't wished you a Merry Christmas."

He smiled. "Uhm, Merry Christmas."

Sophie felt out of breath.

What is he thinking? I can't tell. Is he happy I'm here or am I making the biggest fool of myself?

"Have you—have you had a good Christmas then?" She tried to catch her breath.

"I'm not sure yet." He took a step closer.

"I also realized that I hadn't said a few things that I should've said, like thank you, Max. You helped make the tournament a success in a hundred ways, and I thought you were distracting me, but now I know that what you really did was give me the confidence to see what I want—to see all the things I want—"

"Sophie, stop. Stop right there."

Oh god, what should I do? Should I just leave? Where's a giant meteor hurling to Earth when you need one?

"Stop talking and come here." He held out his hand to her. "Please."

Sophie didn't trust her own legs anymore, but she managed the few steps and then took his hand.

Max pulled her closer and reaching out his index finger slowly traced the contours of her lips. "I don't want to talk anymore."

Max held her face then gave her a long, slow kiss. Sophie melted into him. It felt like floating on the surface of the ocean. She didn't understand the science of how it worked, just that if she let go, somehow, she'd float, and it was bliss.

They parted and he stroked her hair. "I've been dying to do that ever since you burst into my store and started shouting at me. That kiss is probably my favorite Christmas present."

"Probably?" She playfully pulled back a little.

He gave her his mischievous grin. "Technically, Christmas isn't over 'til midnight."

She bit her lip but continued to meet his gaze, still vibrating from the kiss.

"Sophie, I want to invite you in, but I want to get something straight first. I'm not playing games here, Sophie Berlin. I'm not a teenager anymore and I'm not some kid in his twenties that doesn't know what he wants. I don't want to just meet you for coffee or go on an occasional date. I want a real, live relationship with all the trimmings—all the frustrations and all the phenomenal, messy, unpredictable things."

"Love all," Sophie said, smiling.

"I'm not finished. I want to wake up to you in the morning, and I want the smell of your hair to be the last thing I remember before I fall asleep. I want to have lots of short fights with you followed by long makeup sessions. I'm even open to your damn to-do lists! I hope it doesn't scare you, but I'm in love with you. The question is: What do you have to say to that?"

"I say . . . how 'bout we spend the rest of Christmas night by the fire planning Spring Break?"

About the Author

Renata Illustrata is an author, illustrator, and curator of whimsy from the sweet tea–soaked hills of Knoxville, Tennessee. She loves crafting narratives with big heart, big problems, and a witty, whimsical resemblance to real life. When permitted to goof off, Renata enjoys drawing cartoons, designing impertinent T-shirts, late-night baking, and overspending wildly on art supplies.

You can find Renata Illustrata on:
Instagram @renataillustrata

And visit her website at www.renataillustrata.com

ONCE UPON A STORM

Once Upon a Storm

S.B. Rizk

LUNA STARED AT THE CRACKLING flames dancing in the brick fireplace. Nothing beat a warm fire on a cold winter day, but the scent of smoke and burning wood brought her back to memories of sitting around the campfire, roasting marshmallows as a child.

I probably have a book for that, she thought.

Her muscles relaxed as her body melted into Ben's broad chest while he ran his fingers through her curly red hair. She peeked over her shoulder—he rested against the back of the gray loveseat wearing her favorite blue flannel shirt, which made his hazel eyes pop when they were open. His tousled black hair and overgrown beard needed a trim.

Is he falling asleep?

Ben lazily opened one eyelid as if he'd read her thoughts. "What's up, buttercup?"

Luna grinned. "Nothing, I just love you. Get out of my head."

"You better." He leaned in for a kiss, but when they were a breath away from one another, they were startled by the ringing of the brass and ivory antique rotary phone on the small table across the room.

Luna grabbed Ben's wrist, turning it to see his watch.

Who would be calling this late?

She jumped up and ran over to the phone. "Hello?"

Luna jerked the phone away from her ear—the muffled sounds of a hysterical woman came through the receiver loud and clear.

"Jeez, Mom, I think you just blew out my eardrum." She switched hands with the phone and rubbed at her ear. "I need you to slow down and start from the beginning."

"The house is still a disaster, and the repairs won't be finished in time for the Icicle Inn-Cursion. I told your father to leave well enough alone, but oh no, the house *needed* upgrades. This is the only time of the year where I get all of my children together since everyone moved out and I can't believe we will have to skip it this year," her mother said between sniffles on the other end of the line.

Luna shook her head, sighed, and focused on the wall lined with shelves full of books of every size and color from floor to ceiling while her mother let it all out. She often considered arranging them by height or color as some people do, but she found the chaos charming.

"You need to think of a better name for our winter family reunion. Your house isn't an inn. Skipping one year isn't the end of the world. There's always next year."

"Who knows if I'll even be alive for the next one." She started to sob. Loudly.

Luna pulled the receiver away from her ear, counted to sixty, and put it back—her mother's sobs were close to being frenetic.

"Mom."

The wailing got louder.

"You need to—"

She sounded like she was starting to hyperventilate.

Luna rubbed her forehead. "OKAY, I'LL DO IT!"

The other end of the line got quiet before her mother sniffled. "You'll do what, dear?"

"I'll host the winter reunion."

"That's sweet, but I couldn't ask you to do that. It's a lot of work, and if I remember correctly, your house is too small."

"You aren't asking, Mom, I'm offering. It's the best solution since I'm the only one living across town. This way everyone can keep their travel arrangements the same. My house is plenty big enough. I don't think you've even seen all of the rooms since you've never had an official tour any of the times you were here." Luna closed her eyes and rubbed her temple again.

"Are you sure?"

"Yes, I'm sure."

Miraculously, her mother instantly stopped crying and said in a high-pitched voice, "Okay, I'll start making the calls to let everyone know about the change of plans."

The line went dead before Luna could respond. She took a deep breath and faced Ben, who wore an amused look on his face as a smile tugged at his lips.

"You're hosting this year's Icicle Inn-Cursion. Do you think that's smart?"

Luna put her hands on her hips. "Why wouldn't it be smart? Maybe I want my parents and my siblings to come stay with their families."

Or maybe Mom will finally see that I'm not a screw up.

Eleanor had held Luna to a higher standard her entire life as the eldest of her three kids and had been sorely disappointed when she majored in art, unlike her siblings, who went on to major in law and medicine. When Luna announced she planned on opening a florist shop, Petal to the Metal, Eleanor didn't speak to her for weeks. She had insisted that Luna's education had been a waste of time and money and refused to listen to anything about it.

But Eleanor was wrong, and Luna was determined to succeed, and she did. Luckily, her father was the complete opposite of her mother and had been there with Luna every step of the way—from handling the paperwork after she inherited some money from Mrs. Honeycutt, a kind old lady who lived next door to her shop and would come in daily to smell all the flowers until Luna started bringing her some of her own, right down to picking out the wallpaper. Petal to the Metal wasn't your average flower shop. Luna combined her love of flowers with her skills from art school, by handcrafting metal sculptures instead of ordinary vases to house the flowers. Her business had been thriving for almost ten years and was why she was able to purchase her home several years earlier, Eleanor had not once asked how the business was doing or even visited the shop.

"Your family is great, babe, you know I love them. But..." He spread his arms wide and looked around the room.

While it was quiet like this, the room would seem like an ordinary library to someone who didn't know better. Each wall was completely lined with books that extended much higher than they should, considering this was a single-story house. The shelves were so high, in fact, that Luna had to overcome her fear of heights whenever she needed to climb the rickety rolling ladder to reach some of the books.

The charcoal-colored carpet never needed to be vacuumed, no matter what color it decided to take on. There was a foldable cherry desk on the right side of the room that didn't come with the library when Luna bought the house, but she liked it for when she mapped out work projects. On more than one occasion, she had found it in the hallway, banished by the library.

"The last time someone found out about your *little* secret, the house was nearly burned down—with you in it!"

"Don't remind me. I still haven't gotten rid of all of the scorch marks," she grumbled. "Besides, my parents won't try to burn it down. The worst that would happen is my Mom probably calling in an exorcist."

"I don't think you realize how traumatizing finding out is."

"I wasn't traumatized when I found out."

"Yeah, but you like to go with the flow, and some of us like to think more logically."

She chewed her lip and waved her arm. "Pssh, it'll be fine. It's only for a few days. Plus, I've hidden *your* book where no one will come across it, and it took you months to find out even with you being here every day anyways."

He arched an eyebrow. "Alright, if you say so, but that's not all."

Luna cocked her head to the side.

"The Icicle Inn-Cursion is what, six days from now? There isn't enough space for eight extra people to sleep in this house. Where do you intend to put them all?"

A wide smile spread across her face. She pulled up the sleeves of her beige knitted sweater as she walked over to a shelf and ran her finger along the spines, careful not to displace the string of vines sprinkled with light purple bunches of wisteria that hung throughout the shelf ends and breaks in the books, going down the row until she came to a stop. Delicately, she lifted a fat book from the shelf and held it out for Ben to see.

The glow from the fireplace illuminated the room just enough to reveal the outline of a house on the cover and the words *Expand Your Home*.

Ben laughed. "Alright, whatever you say, but I don't want to hear any complaints when someone in your family needs therapy from being terrorized by your library. Now, can you please get back over here? I was quite comfortable before the phone rang."

Giggling, she dropped the book on the oval, mahogany table in the center of the room and leaped onto the loveseat, into his lap, pulling the wool, maroon blanket over them. "You know what would make this better?"

He put a finger to his chin, pretending to think it over. "Hot cocoa?"

By the time she grinned and nodded, two steaming mugs of hot cocoa overflowing with marshmallows appeared on the table before them.

Ben picked up the mugs, handing one to her. "Would you look at that? You didn't even have to open a book that time."

Cradling the navy ceramic mug in both hands, Luna took a slow sip and looked up at Ben with chocolate and melted marshmallows on her upper lip.

"Ask and you shall receive. I don't know if I'll ever get the hang of it, but the library seems to be able to handle most things to do with comfort on its own."

They spent the rest of the evening laughing over bottomless mugs of hot cocoa and planning what they would do for the rest of the winter season.

Luna inhaled the savory smell of beef and herbs as she stood by the kitchen door, swirling her glass of pink Moscato.

Ben tugged at the white apron that covered his black sweater and khakis as he leaned over the large pot of bubbling beef stew on the stove. "It doesn't need any more pepper; it's fine the way it is."

"Is everything alright in here?" She took a sip of wine.

"Everything would be great if Cookie would stop trying to add more pepper to my stew," he said, placing a glass pepper shaker, next to three other pepper shakers in front of a propped-open cookbook.

The pages of the book riffled, and Ben held up his hands in surrender. "Sorry. *Our* stew."

Luna smiled behind her glass before sipping when something on the metal shelf above the stove caught her eye.

"Ben," she said with a quick nod toward the shelf.

He turned around and lunged forward, catching the newest pepper shaker that had wobbled off, almost landing in the pot.

DING-DONG!

"They're here!" Luna placed her glass on the marble countertop and straightened her yellow blouse. "Why don't you put Cookie away so she doesn't get in any more trouble out here, and can you please make sure I put the other book up on the display stand? I can't remember if I moved it off the table or not."

The cookbook slammed itself closed, and all the extra pepper shakers disappeared.

"Sure thing, babe," he said as he gently picked up the tattered, brown book and headed for the library.

As Luna walked to the front door, she could hear him whispering, "If you would have just let go of the pepper thing, you could have stayed out here with everyone."

When she opened the eggplant-colored door, a strong gust of wind brought the freezing air in to nip her exposed skin. With a wide smile, she held her arms open, ready to embrace her parents.

Her mother stopped blowing into her hands as she rubbed them together and stepped forward, pulling Luna into a tight hug.

"Hi, Mom. Could you ease up a bit? You're squeezing pretty tight."

"I wasn't squeezing. It must be the few extra pounds you've put on this year."

Luna tried to hide the flash of hurt on her face.

When she was released, she gave her father a half hug while he kissed her head.

"You look beautiful, honey."

"Thanks, Dad," she said in a small voice.

As the three of them stepped inside, her mother asked, "Notice anything different?"

Luna looked her mother up and down. She wore black boots lined with white faux fur, jeans, and a navy parka. Her emerald eyes, which mirrored Luna's, opened wider as she impatiently tapped her foot.

"You cut your hair!" Luna touched the tips of her mother's new bob, her usually curly, red hair hung very straight and much shorter than ever.

"What do you think?" She tilted her head, modeling her new hair.

"It looks great."

"Charles, Eleanor, how have you been?" Ben swooped in and embraced both of them before looking pointedly at Eleanor.

"I love what you've done with your hair. Let me take those," he said, reaching for the brown leather suitcases Charles held.

Eleanor beamed, looked at Luna, and lifted an eyebrow. "Have I told you I like this one?"

"Only, like, every time you see him." She looked over her mother's shoulder at Ben, who winked and blew a kiss.

"Have you been taking care of my daughter?" Charles asked, putting on his best stern face.

Luna stifled a giggle. Her dad put on a good front, but he was a big softie.

"Of course, sir," Ben said.

"Very good. What's for dinner? Something smells delicious." Charles clapped a hand on Ben's shoulder before pulling off his black parka and handing it to Luna, who hung it, along with Eleanor's, on the coat rack by the front door.

"Why don't you come and see for yourself while I get you a drink?" Ben said, striding toward the kitchen.

Charles started to follow but was stopped by Eleanor. "Just a moment dear." She fixed the collar of his green Oxford.

"Thanks." He pulled his fingers through his graying hair as he trailed behind Ben, who insisted he could carry the bags himself.

"Have you spoken to Emily or Little Charles?" Luna asked.

"You know he hates being called that," Eleanor scolded.

"I know, I know." She wagged a finger.

As she opened her mouth, a squeaky voice behind her mocked, "I'm not little, I'm a grown man."

"Emily!" Eleanor squealed and was nearly knocked over by her grandchildren, Lucas and Tiffany, who she hadn't noticed racing toward her in their excitement to hug her.

"Gram!" they screamed as they both wrapped their arms around a watery-eyed Eleanor.

"Look how much you two have grown," she said, taking them in as they stepped back.

She put a hand over each of their heads, hovering over their dark hair. "No, you couldn't possibly be my grandchildren. You are far too tall."

They giggled, and meanwhile, Luna hugged her sister. "Always with the grand entrance."

Emily furrowed her eyebrows. "We just knocked at the wrong door. There's nothing grand about it."

"Where is Caleb?"

"He dragged Ben out the back door to grab the bags before Mom saw him." Emily pulled off her white hat, allowing thick, titian hair to fall to her shoulders, and moved to take off her cream-colored peacoat, stopping as she eyed the full coat rack.

"Maybe you could show us to our rooms?"

On cue, Ben came stumbling in the front door, arms full of colorful luggage, embroidered with the kids' names.

"Of course, follow us," she said before leading everyone down the hallway and coming to a stop by the library door, which felt out of place.

Unlike the rest of the doors in the house, this one had a rounded arch and was made of almost ancient-looking wood that was split in many places and carved with leaves and vines crawling along the edges. It had a black, oval handle with a skeleton keyhole underneath and looked like something out of a fairytale.

Luna and Ben placed their phones in the wicker basket on the round, white oak table outside the library under a sign that read, "Shh, your phone needs some quiet time, too." She grabbed the cool handle, took a deep breath while saying a silent prayer to herself, and pushed the door open.

All seemed calm in the room; the only noises to be heard were the chafing sounds of their feet as they walked onto the carpet.

"Beanbags! Auntie Luna, these are awesome!" Lucas yelled as he and Tiffany rushed by the adults and plopped onto the two oversized electric blue beanbag chairs on the left side of the room beside the table with the antique rotary phone.

A large sky-blue sectional, with tangerine throw pillows, took up the right side of the room in front of the fireplace. The shelves on the wall to the left of the fireplace were lined with books and small vases arranged with orange and white flowers. There was a break in the shelves large enough for a simple red door before wrapping around to the next wall, where there was a break for a second red door.

That's odd. There should be three.

"I never knew you had a library!" Eleanor swatted Luna's arm as she passed her, with Charles close behind.

"Really? The library is the reason I bought the house," Luna muttered.

Her parents took the door to the left on the fireplace wall, leaving Emily with the other.

Luna and Ben smiled when they heard Eleanor scream in delight, just before she came running back into the library to grab them in a one-armed hug.

"Thank you so much! I don't know how you managed it, but it's a nearly perfect replica of our room at home."

Ben opened his mouth, but no words came out, so Luna put a hand on his arm before rubbing the back of his head. "Yeah, well I know how much you love hosting the Inn-Cursion so I tried to bring a little bit of home here."

Eleanor lovingly cupped Luna's cheek and retreated to her room to unpack. Luna and Ben walked over to the doorway for a better view of her parents smiling and laughing as they transferred clothes from the brown suitcases into the dresser.

"I thought the Inn-Cursion was only a few days. Are they planning on moving in?" Ben whispered.

Luna giggled. "No. Mom says when you live out of your luggage, you feel more like a guest and family should always feel at home."

"I want the top bunk!"

"No way, it's mine!" the children screamed from Emily's room.

Still holding the kids' duffle bags, Ben squeezed into their room and placed the bags on the floor in front of an impressive twin-sized bunk bed. A red plastic slide connected to the top bunk made for an easy exit from the bed.

Tiffany blocked the top of the ladder on the opposite side, claiming the top for herself, as Lucas stood with his arms crossed, frowning and sticking his tongue out at her.

Emily and Caleb discarded their coats, hanging them from the hooks on the closet door by their queen-sized four-poster bed as they ignored the bickering.

Ben crouched beside Lucas and put a hand on his shoulder. "I know the ladder is cool, but check this out. Why don't you hop on the bottom bunk?"

Lucas flung his arms down to his side with clenched fists. "No way! If I get on the bottom, Tiffany will say that I have to keep it."

Ben chuckled. "Just trust me."

Lucas looked from the bottom bunk to the top, and then back at Ben. He slightly shook his head and quietly said, "Okay."

On the frame above the bottom bunk, where the bed was positioned against the wall, an indigo curtain hung that Ben pulled around the frame, encasing Lucas in his own private space.

"Neat! A fort!" he screamed, peeking his head out. "Thanks, Ben!"

Nosy faces peeked in through the door. Eleanor leaned over Luna's shoulder, attempting to whisper, "And he's good with kids. What are you waiting for?"

"Ma!" Luna shook her head.

"I wish I had a bed that awesome," said a husky voice behind Luna and Eleanor.

They both jumped. "Charlie!"

He hugged Luna and kissed their mother on the cheek.

"Where's Natalie? And how did you get in?" Luna asked.

"She's back at the hotel nursing a migraine, but she'll be by tomorrow. You left the front door unlocked."

"What do you mean by hotel? You guys aren't staying here?"

Charlie wrapped an arm over Luna's shoulder. "Listen, I love you guys and I'm so excited to catch up, but I need some alone time with my wife."

"Yeah, you can be *alone* in the room I set up for you here," Luna huffed.

"Oh, leave him alone, they're still in their honeymoon phase," Emily cooed.

"Luna wouldn't know about that, dear, she's still living in sin," Eleanor said.

Luna rolled her eyes. "Finished unpacking already, Mom?"

"Yes, once I got over my surprise at how well the room was set up, I could have unpacked blindfolded."

Everyone's attention was drawn to Tiffany when she asked, "Why is there a crib in here?"

Emily blanched at the sight of the white, wicker bassinet in the corner of the room but Caleb quickly said, "That must be for your baby doll. Auntie Luna really thought of everything."

After a hectic dinner with the additional company of Aunt Beth, Uncle Lenny, and cousin Leona, and the chaos that came with escorting the non-overnight guests out and making sure everyone else went to their rooms, Luna gratefully retired to her room with Ben. Once her bedroom door closed, Luna stood in the middle of the room with her eyes shut and took deep breaths.

Ben came up behind her and began rubbing the knots out of her shoulder. "Relax, babe, you are wicked tense."

"I know. I love having them here, but Mom gets under my skin with all of her little comments, and I forgot how busy a full house can be." She rolled her head, stretching her neck.

He rubbed harder against a stubborn knot. "Your mom means well, but if it'll relieve some of your stress, I'll try to keep her busy when I can for you. And hey, day one is over and there weren't any casualties. Besides, we usually have a bunch of strange, fuzzy creatures running around the house and stubborn books sneaking out of the library. I think we can handle your family for a few more days."

Luna stilled at the mention of fuzzy creatures. "Oh no, I didn't even think about that. What if something gets loose while they're here?"

Ben tugged on her shoulder, and when Luna turned to face him, he cupped her cheeks and looked straight into her tired emerald eyes. "We will be extra vigilant and just hope that if something does decide to explore the house, it's not another dragon."

Luna wrapped her arms around him and put her head on his chest. "If you're trying to make me feel better, you aren't doing a great job."

He kissed her forehead. "One of these days, you're going to have to accept that you can't control everything, especially when you make impulsive decisions."

Rolling her eyes, Luna changed into her favorite gray pajamas covered with fat pink cats and matching fuzzy socks. Ben busied himself lighting the pine-scented candles along the dressers and windowsill. He flicked the light switch and Luna plopped on the bed just as there were three soft taps at the door. Ben pulled it open and revealed an irritated-looking Emily.

"Can I talk to my sister?"

"Sure thing," Ben said, opening the door wider and stepping aside.

As Emily passed him, Ben looked at Luna and said, "I'm just going to give the house a quick walkthrough while you guys talk."

When he closed the door, Emily turned on Luna. "Uh, what the hell were you thinking with the crib? That wasn't funny. I don't know how you found out, but Mom and Dad don't know yet."

Scrunching her face, Luna stood up. "What are you—"

Right then, Luna recalled Emily's pale face at the sight of the bassinet in the bedroom the house had conjured for her and Caleb.

"Are you pregnant?"

"What do you mean *am I pregnant*? Of course I am, and based on your stupid prank, you already knew that," she said as she paced the room.

"I didn't, but the library did," Luna mumbled.

"What was that?"

Luna sighed. "I said I didn't. It was an oversight. Old furniture left by the previous owners. I just never got rid of it and forgot about it."

Emily stilled and looked her in the face.

"Damn. I'm sorry. I thought it was your big sisterly way of getting me to come clean to our folks."

She shook her head. They stared at one another in awkward silence while Emily rubbed the back of her neck.

"Now that it's out in the open," Luna said gently, "congratulations? I can't believe I'm getting another niece or nephew."

Emily's shoulders fell along with her defenses, and she welcomed the hug Luna offered.

As they hugged, Emily said, "Thanks but can we keep this between us for now? I know Mom is going to tell me I should have stopped at two, I already have a boy and a girl, and I just want to enjoy this for a little longer."

"Of course, but I don't think she'll say that. I think it's more likely that she'll say 'See, Luna, your sister is having her third child when you haven't even had one yet.'"

They laughed, and as Emily walked out the door, Luna said, "Tell Caleb congrats for me."

"I will."

Luna sat at the kitchen table listening to the bacon and sausage sizzle while she watched Ben expertly maneuver around the stove. Seeing him in his element fascinated her. She used to try and help more with meals, but even with Cookie's guidance, that always ended in disaster. Luckily, when Ben finally came to terms with all of the weird stuff that happened around here because of the library, he and Cookie became pretty much inseparable. Luna had no complaints; the dishes Ben and Cookie created together were addicting. So aside from occasionally grabbing something for Ben, they agreed that she would let him handle the food, especially when they had company.

"Luna, dear, do you need help with anything?" Eleanor appeared in the kitchen.

Stopping short in the doorway, she frowned at Luna and said, "Poor Ben, she has you cooking again? Why don't you relax with Charles in the parlor and I'll finish up here."

"No, thanks, I'm fine here," he said as he turned the sausages over with his tongs.

"Oh, nonsense, you work too hard. At least step aside and let me help."

Eleanor stepped up to the stove and nudged him over.

Ben paused before making space for her—not long enough for Eleanor to catch on, but Luna knew he struggled with the decision and sooner than later he would regret giving in.

Eleanor cranked the heat up on all the burners. "You have the heat too low; it's going to take forever this way."

Luna giggled at the look of sheer horror that overtook Ben's face, and Cookie flopped hard on her back, open, landing with a loud *thunk* that made Eleanor jump.

Leaving Ben with his dramatic book and her overbearing mother to fend for himself, Luna followed a rhythmic thumping into the dining room where Lucas and Tiffany sat across from each other, still wearing their matching black and red pajamas. Tiffany swung her feet, the left one repeatedly bumping against the leg of the chair, and Lucas teetered in his, looking up at the ceiling.

"What are you all up to?"

Tiffany stopped swinging her feet. "Mom and Dad told us to wait out here for breakfast to be done, so they could both make work calls, but we're *so* bored, Auntie Luna."

Luna peeked back in on the trainwreck in the kitchen and then smiled at the children. "Want to do something fun?"

"Duh," Lucas said, finally acknowledging her presence.

She led the two very unimpressed children into the library.

With a disgusted look, Lucas said, "You want us to read! This is supposed to be a vacation."

"Oh, I love books with pretty pictures. Do you have any with ponies?" Tiffany asked.

Stifling a giggle, Luna said, "I'm sure I have a book with ponies around here somewhere, but no, Lucas, I didn't bring you in here just to read."

She walked past the now white sectional, whose throw pillows had changed into a shimmery silver, and stopped by the bookshelf next to the window.

"Did you know books are like magic?" she asked, pulling thin, colorful books out, checking the illustrations on the cover, and placing them back.

"They are?" Tiffany asked, her golden eyes wide.

"They are. When you read, you can be anyone and travel anywhere. Ah hah!"

She walked to them with the book she had been looking for.

"And sometimes they can even bring some of those places or things to you."

She held up a book with a picture of a fat snowman wearing a black hat surrounded by children—exaggeratedly big snowflakes fell around them.

Lucas frowned. "I wish it were snowing here. Mom told us all about the epic snowball fights you guys had when you were younger. She said Uncle Charlie made snowballs super-fast and was always the champ, but I bet I could beat him."

"And sledding! Is it true that Gram and Pa used to take you sledding at a hill that was taller than your house?" Tiffany asked, wide eyed.

"It certainly felt that way." Luna smiled.

Lucas walked over to the window and pointed outside. "What kind of winter is this, when there's no snow?"

"You're right! Let's see if we can change that." She tousled his hair and placed the book open on the table.

Tiffany excitedly flipped the pages as a scowling Lucas stood behind her. Luna stood in place, watching them, patiently waiting for what she hoped would happen.

Lucas touched his hand to his cheek and rubbed his fingers together, looking around the room.

"Is everything alright?" Luna asked.

"Yes, I just felt something wet on my cheek."

"Me too!" Tiffany said.

Specks of white floated down from the ceiling, so spread out and slow at first that the kids had no clue what was happening. They began to fall faster and grew larger. The next one that landed on Lucas's face didn't melt upon contact.

Tiffany pointed at him. "There's a snowflake on your face!"

Opening his mouth to protest, Lucas pointed at her curly, dark brown hair, which was now dusted with soft, white flakes. "There's some on you, too!"

They spread their arms and twirled in circles with their tongues out. The rug had become a shade of light gray, which blended in perfectly with the growing piles of snow.

"I'm going to make a snow angel!" Lucas spread out on the ground in the empty space where the beanbag chairs were before, unaware they were gone.

"Me, too!" Tiffany followed suit.

They laughed as they furiously moved their arms and legs, trying to outdo each other.

Luna jumped when she heard: "Wow, they've come a long way with the fake snow standard since we were kids. It even feels cold."

Emily stood in her bedroom doorway wearing an oversized white, knitted sweater and blue leggings, watching the snow land on her outstretched hand.

So she does know how to relax.

"I know, right?"

"Do you remember that first year it didn't snow, and we were bummed we couldn't have our snowball fight, so Dad got the instant snow that tasted like soap and turned the parlor into a winter wonderland?"

Luna laughed so hard her stomach cramped. "And Mom was so mad at him. It took weeks for her to get all of it out of the furniture."

Caleb joined in on the fun, wearing the worst ugly sweater Luna had ever seen. It was different shades of brown, and the patterns looked like something that belonged to a ninety-year-old man. He squeezed in beside his children on the floor, who then decided it would be more fun to bury him in the snow—they started with his bald head.

"Breakfast is ready," Ben's voice echoed down the hallway.

Emily and Caleb started dusting the kids off. Ben's face fell when he opened the door, and he scrambled to get out of the way as the children barreled out of the room. Caleb and Emily followed behind, laughing.

Emily stopped and looked around the room. Snow was steadily

falling and was about midway up the calf by now. "Do you want me to help clean this up?"

"No thanks, I got it." Luna nodded toward the hall where enthusiastic voices all speaking over one another were coming from. "Besides, it sounds like it's all hands on deck out there."

"You're probably right." Emily laughed.

Ben waited for Emily to be out of sight before he stepped inside the room and closed the door. "What happened?"

Luna shrugged. "The kids were bored."

"And how do they think all of this happened?" He waved his arm around.

She walked over to the table and picked up the open book while brushing the snow off of the pages. "I told them books are magic."

Luna snapped the book closed and, just like that, the snow was gone, and the library was dry and warm, as if nothing had happened.

After returning the book to its place on the shelf, she walked over to Ben and said, "Relax, my sister thought it was instant snow. And even if the kids do tell anyone, who is going to believe that a magic book made it snow inside of my library?"

Speechless, he stood with his mouth open. She got on tiptoes and kissed his cheek before heading for the kitchen.

The house smelled like hickory bacon and maple syrup and the dining room was loud with excited voices. Luna walked flat against the wall into the room looking for an empty chair at the long walnut table. There was usually more space, but they had to install the leaf so all ten place settings would fit. True to his word, Charlie and Natalie showed up to join them for breakfast right as Ben was bringing the food to the dining room.

Luna found a seat between Eleanor and Natalie. Ben sat up at the other end near Emily and the kids. Luna reached over the table, piling a little of everything onto her plate—there was sausage, bacon, pancakes, and scrambled eggs, and she didn't know where to start.

"You know, dear, if you can't be bothered to take on any of the domestic responsibilities, then you should at least watch your figure," Eleanor whispered.

Luna lowered her face, taking slow, even breaths as she tried to calm herself. She pushed her food around the plate, having lost her appetite, and sat quietly for most of breakfast, just listening to everyone around her.

Thump. Thump. Thump.

"What's that banging?" Tiffany asked. Most of the other adults, except for Ben, were too wrapped up in their conversations to pay attention.

Lucas kneeled beside the walnut china cabinet. "I think it's coming from here."

He opened the doors, and a fat raccoon wearing a pink collar with a split ear came tumbling out, holding a teacup. Eleanor and Emily screamed bloody murder and began throwing glasses and silverware at the creature. The raccoon wove in and out of chair legs and feet as it fled. Charlie grabbed the spatula from beside the stack of pancakes and chased after the beast, screaming profanities.

Ben ran both of his hands down his face and then got up to chase after Charlie. On his way out, he gave Luna a panicked look that said, *What do we do now?* Luna dropped her head on the table too aggressively, connecting with a painful *thump*. She knew Charlie wouldn't catch the raccoon. The number of times the damn thing got loose in the house and evaded her and Ben was almost embarrassing.

Lucas laughed at all the commotion, and Caleb comforted a teary-eyed Tiffany, who was upset with Uncle Charlie for chasing the raccoon away.

"I think it escaped from whatever hole it got in through. I can't find it anywhere," Charlie said breathlessly as he plopped back into his seat.

"Don't worry about it, man. I'll put a call in to animal control," Ben said, sliding into his seat.

It took a few minutes for everyone to compose themselves enough to get back to their food. Eleanor was noticeably jumpy at every little movement.

"With proper housekeeping that thing never would have gotten in here. Who knows what diseases it has and what it may have contaminated? No wonder Benjamin hasn't proposed yet." Eleanor wagged her finger at Luna.

Luna slammed her hands on the table and stood. "Get off my back, would you? I've gone out of my way to host because *you* just had to have your family get-together or you would have *died*, and you've done nothing but nag me and put me down since you got here, as usual."

Eleanor's hand flew to her chest, and she recoiled as if she had been struck.

"Hey, why don't you take it easy?" Charlie said.

"Take it easy? How am I supposed to take it easy between Mom on my back, Emily accusing me of childish pranks to out her pregnancy, and now there's freaking animals running through the house," she retorted in a frustrated tone.

Emily's face went scarlet, and Luna could picture steam coming from her ears. She looked around the silent room.

Oh, crap.

Emily stalked out of the room. And one by one everyone followed.

The house was eerily quiet for the rest of the day. Everyone spent the time between meals in their rooms. During dinner, the air was thick with tension—it was as if they were scared to even breathe too loud, like doing so would break the delicate peace in the house, and no one was ready to discuss the events of that morning. Charlie and Natalie retreated to their hotel and had dinner there. Luna couldn't blame them.

Several times throughout the day, Luna started to seek out Emily and Caleb but didn't, out of fear of possibly making it worse. She felt awful for revealing their secret. Eleanor's prodding had cracked something inside her, but she knew that was no excuse. As bad as Luna felt, she had no plans to apologize to her mother.

Long after Ben fell asleep that night, Luna tossed and turned, scenes from that morning replaying in her head. She felt icky. Luna hated fighting with people; it always made her stomach hurt.

Just woman up and say sorry to make the peace. There are still a few days left and I will not let this year's blasted Icicle Inn-Cursion be ruined. Mom will hold it over me for the rest of my life.

Luna was ripped from thoughts of how the conversations would go the next day by bloodcurdling screams.

"Lucas? Tiffany?" She shot up in bed. "Something's wrong!" she said, shaking Ben, and bolted out of the room.

As she neared the library door, the children's screams were drowned out by furniture crashing and howling winds. The door wouldn't open no matter how hard she pushed on it.

"Get out of the way," Ben shouted as he raced down the hall, waving her to the side.

The door flew open when he slammed into it. When he regained his footing, they both froze in place, Luna with her hand over her mouth. The thick sheets of snow coming down whirled around the room by vicious winds, along with the furniture that smashed into pieces against the wall. Mounds of snow, easily to the hip, grew around the room. The bookshelves were nearly empty, some books flying through the air and others no doubt buried in snow.

It took a minute for Luna to get eyes on the kids, but when she did, she sprang into action.

"Ben!" She pointed them out.

Lucas was almost upside-down, struggling to hold onto the mantle of the fireplace as his body was being pulled into the air, and Tiffany had both arms tightly squeezed around Lucas's legs. They looked like they would fly away any minute. Luna's heart stopped. While the library fixed most things when you close a book, she had never tested it out with any injuries.

Luna and Ben dove into the snow, shoveling handfuls out of the way, as they looked for the open book.

"Kids, where did you put the book down when you opened it?" Luna yelled.

"What?" they asked.

"Why does that matter? The storm would have blown it into a different spot by now," Ben said in a raised voice.

Luna shook her head. "No, it doesn't work that way. The magic doesn't disturb the book it came from. The book will be wherever they left it."

She cupped her mouth with her hands and screamed over the roaring wind, "Where did you put the book?"

The muffled response could hardly be heard.

"What!"

She and Ben squinted as they listened—they couldn't rely on lip reading to help make out the words since the visibility got worse by the second.

Again a muffled response came through: "John the grouch?"

Then it clicked—they looked at each other and said in unison, "On the couch!"

They trudged through to the area where the sectional should be, but the white appearance it had taken on earlier helped it camouflage with the piles of snow.

After moments of walking in circles, Ben accidentally kicked the couch. "Oof. I found it!"

They dug through the snow, blindly pulling free any book they touched. Finally, Luna pulled out an open book by the back cover and slammed it shut, not taking the time to brush the snow off it.

The room went silent—Lucas and Tiffany landed on the floor with a hard *thud*. The snow was gone, the no-longer broken furniture put back in its place, and all the books, except for the one Luna held, were safely on the shelves. She saw the words *Devastating Storms* on the cover before placing it in a space on one of the higher shelves.

"Are you two okay?" Ben asked, helping them off the floor.

"I think so," Tiffany said.

Luna crouched in front of them. "What were you thinking? You could have been seriously hurt."

Tiffany swayed and put her head down as Lucas said, "We were so bored all day, stuck in the room with our parents. I tried finding the book you had earlier, but there are a lot of books in here."

Luna tried to hide her smile. "Yeah, there are."

"Then I found that one and there was a picture with snow on the back cover so I thought it would work. I'm sorry. Please don't be mad at us."

"I could never be mad at you. I'm just glad you're okay." Luna pulled them both in for a hug. "I'm the one who should say sorry. It's my fault you guys ended up stuck in the room. I made everything awkward around here when I lost my temper this morning."

"Are you going to tell Mom and Dad?" Tiffany whispered.

Oh crap, their parents! Emily should be out here any minute ready to kill us.

Luna pursed her lips. "I'll make you a deal. We can keep this between us if you promise not to touch any of the books in here without supervision."

Tiffany and Lucas shared a look and then stuck out their hands. "Deal."

Relieved that the children were unharmed, Luna stood up.

"Babe, we have a problem."

The shelves on the fireplace wall extended down, with no interruptions. The bedroom doors were gone. One look at the shelf where the home book had been displayed showed an empty stand. Luna's stomach bottomed out and she took large gulps of air, struggling to breathe.

Ben squeezed her shoulder, "We'll find it."

She scratched her head. "I don't understand. It should have been put back where it was when I closed the other book."

"Maybe it ended up on one of the shelves since it's not usually on the stand," Ben said.

Chewing her lip, she took a deep breath and said, "Okay."

They instructed the children to sit on the sectional and not touch anything as they combed through the books. With each passing minute that they didn't find the one they were looking for, Luna's panic became evident. She no longer took care with each book and started ripping them from the shelves, tossing them aside when they weren't the right ones.

With both hands on her hips, Luna looked around the room at empty shelves. All of the books were in scattered piles around the room.

She felt woozy; blackness crept to the edge of her vision as she pulled at her hair. "It's not here! What should I do? They're gone."

Luna spiraled her way into a panic attack, clutching at her chest and hyperventilating as the kids watched.

Ben rubbed her back. "Look at me."

Tears welled in her eyes. "I never apologized. They are all still mad at me."

Ben tilted Luna's face to him. "Don't worry, you aren't getting out of apologizing that easily. We will figure this out. But I need you to calm down; you aren't going to be able to help if you keep freaking out. And you're scaring the kids."

She closed her eyes and took a deep breath in through her nose, out through her mouth—repeating this until her breathing slowed to almost normal.

Clapping her hands together, she said, "It's been a long time since dinner, and I don't think very clearly when I'm hungry. How about we go into the kitchen to get a snack?

"Do you have cinnamon rolls?" Tiffany squeaked.

"I want chips," Lucas said.

"We have whatever you guys want."

They rushed into the kitchen, where a tray of cinnamon rolls and potato chips sat on the counter next to the open cookbook.

"Hey, how'd you do that so fast?" Lucas asked, grabbing his chips to go to the dining room.

Luna and Ben still stuttered over their words, trying to come up with something other than *magic books*, when they all took their seats at the table.

Thump. Thump Thump.

Momentarily saved by the cabinet, Luna thought with a sigh.

Ben frowned as he opened the door. The raccoon sat inside on top of a pile of stolen items, holding a sneaker with teeth marks on the tongue.

"You're okay!" Tiffany exclaimed.

"Wait a second." Luna opened the other cabinet door, and on top of a second pile of stolen goods was a familiar book with a house.

She gingerly picked up the book as if it were going to crumble into a pile of ashes. When it didn't, she hugged it tight to her chest.

"I'll be back," she said to Ben, and then to the raccoon, "I'll deal with you later when I find your book."

Dragging her feet to the library, her legs felt like lead.

What if this doesn't work? What if they aren't in the rooms anymore and are trapped in the book? How would I get them out? What if the wrong rooms appear?

Too many horrible possibilities swirled through her mind. She opened the book to the section about adding rooms and closed her eyes. When she opened them, two doors, identical to the original ones, were back in the same places along the walls.

Luna propped the book on the display stand and walked to the closest door—her parents' room.

"Please be in here, please be in here," she chanted.

The door creaked as she opened it enough to peek inside. Her parents soundly slept—Eleanor laid on her side, wearing a red mask with cartoonish eyes over her own, and Charles on his back, with his mouth open wide, the light reflecting off of the drool dribbling down his chin.

Luna could finally take a full breath. She checked the other two rooms, making sure everyone was where they were supposed to be. Ben, Lucas, and Tiffany entered the library, walking through the maze of piles of discarded books from the search. The kids yawned and rubbed their eyes.

"I think these two should be off to bed, if everything is all set," Ben said, with a hand on each of their shoulders.

"Of course." Luna smiled. "Goodnight, see you in the morning."

"Goodnight," two small, tired voices echoed.

Luna woke up bright and early. She skipped to the kitchen and pulled out the eggs, milk, butter, and bread, placing them on the counter next to the cookbook. As she reached for the milk to whisk in with the eggs, she noticed two new ingredients, cinnamon and sugar.

She smiled at the book. "You are absolutely right, Cookie."

The french toast sizzled, and the smell of cinnamon floated through the air.

"That smells delicious, Benjamin. What are you—" Eleanor stopped when she spotted Luna.

When Luna opened her mouth to say something, Eleanor held up her hand.

"Let me go first. I'm sorry."

"Huh?"

"You're right. I'm sorry. I never meant to put you down or make you feel bad. I want what's best for you. I've projected my own insecurities onto you, and that was awful of me. You are so beautiful just the way you are. And anyone can see how much you love Ben, but I was raised in a different time. I sometimes forget that domestic responsibilities are shared now. The truth is I'm so proud of you, and I'm angry with myself for making you feel otherwise."

"If you're proud of me then why have you never visited my shop or even asked how it was going?"

Eleanor waved her off. "Dear, your father talks about your shop nonstop every time he drives by it, so I've never felt the need to ask. I did visit it, once, shortly after you opened it. I saw you through the window, arranging an owl piece with carnations dyed a light blue. You looked so happy, and I knew you had made the right choices. We hadn't spoken about the subject for a long time, so I was afraid if I went inside, I would taint your happy space with some of that negativity, even if I didn't mean for it to happen. I got in my car, drove home, and never told your father."

"You came to my shop? And all of this time you let me think you didn't care."

"That was never my intention. It was selfish of me to not try harder to understand and support you. It's been weighing on my mind for a long time, but I could never find the right way to bring it up and you never said anything, so I was hoping maybe our relationship wasn't that broken and that I was being as hard on myself as I was on you."

Luna covered and uncovered her face with her hands. "Of course I never said anything! All I wanted was your approval! I walked on eggshells for years trying to please you. I figured since I wasn't willing to give up my plans for myself, I could at least try my best to not argue with you, but it was still never good enough."

"I can see that now, and I'm *so* sorry. I would give anything to be able to go back and be a better mother, but I can't. All I can do is try to be better moving forward. If it's not too late, I'd like to try to fix things."

Luna turned away from Eleanor, needing the space to think for a minute. Memories of all the times she needed a loving mother to just sit there with her and listen to her ramble about a good day or cry about a bad one resurfaced. Now that she'd finally stood up to her mother, she knew she shouldn't cave in, but a stronger part of her wondered . . . what if they really could fix their relationship?

"I don't know if you can, ten years is a long time, but . . . I'm willing to try," she said as she turned to face her mother.

When Eleanor moved to take a step toward her, Luna took a step back and said, "This doesn't mean I forgive you, and from this day on, if you start back up with the nasty remarks, I'll cut ties with you. I'm at a good place in my life right now, and I don't need anyone, especially my mother, bringing me down."

"I understand," Eleanor hugged her and said, "I love you."

"I love you, too."

As Eleanor pulled back from Luna, she wiped at her watery eyes before the tears could fall. "You should go talk to Emily before we all sit down for breakfast."

"I know. Would you mind taking over here?"

"I thought you'd never ask," Eleanor said, swatting at Luna's backside. "Oh, I called your brother and told him to get his butt back over here. This is still a family vacation."

Luna softly knocked on Emily's door, almost hoping they wouldn't answer. When the door didn't open after a moment, she started to walk away but stopped when she heard a creak. A surprised-looking Caleb stood in the doorway. Momentarily speechless, Luna stumbled over her words. "Is Emily here? I mean, of course she is, can I speak to her?"

"Sure." Caleb further opened the door.

"Actually, I need to speak to both of you."

Caleb walked into the room and stood beside his wife, who frowned at Luna with her arms crossed.

Luna rubbed the back of her neck. "I'm so sorry I told everyone about the baby. I'm not going to waste your time with excuses of me being angry, I was wrong. That wasn't my news to share. I hope you two can forgive me."

Silence.

Caleb looked to Emily, who unblinkingly stared at her sister.

When neither of them said anything, Luna said, "That's all I had to say. Sorry for bothering you."

Chewing on her lip, she backed out of the room. When she reached the doorway, Emily said, "Yeah, you were wrong. That was really shitty of you. But if I'm being honest, I feel a little relieved the secret is out. We are so damn happy, and it was getting so hard not to talk about it."

Luna smiled, "Really? I mean, it is pretty awesome news."

Emily arched an eyebrow. "You lost our trust. I can't foresee us sharing any more secrets with you anytime soon, but—" She looked at Caleb, who nodded. "We forgive you."

Unable to contain herself, Luna ran forward and gave them each a hug. She put her arm over Emily's shoulder and said, "I also came to tell you breakfast is ready—gotta feed my niece or nephew."

The air felt lighter as everyone smiled and laughed over breakfast. Ben must have found the raccoon's book, because he made no appearances, although Luna had checked the china cabinet before everyone took their seats.

As the final forks clinked against the plates and everyone sat back in their chairs with full stomachs, Luna wiped her mouth and stood. "Rest up, everyone, after I'm finished with the dishes, I have a fun activity planned for you all."

On her way out of the dining room, she gave Ben a nod—their signal for him to put their plan into place. She carried a stack of plates into the kitchen and her mother followed, insisting on at least drying and putting them away for her.

Mom just can't help herself.

Once the dishes were done and the surfaces were all wiped down, Luna led everyone to the library.

As they stood by the closed door, Luna placed her phone in the wicker basket on the small table beside Ben's.

"Um, no offense, sis, but we all spent more than enough time cooped in our rooms yesterday, so I hope that isn't where you're bringing us."

Luna swatted Emily's arm.

They all squinted when she pushed the door open. The library was so bright, covered in white as snowflakes gently fell from the ceiling. The room was slightly colder than the rest of the house, and a few inches of snow had collected on the ground and the sectional. Ben stood in the middle of the room with a bag full of gloves.

While there were a few "ooh"s and "aww"s from the adults, the children took advantage of their astonishment and began throwing somewhat unformed snowballs at them after grabbing gloves from Ben.

"Snowball fight!" Lucas screamed.

Everyone else raced in and broke off into groups, except for Charles, who stood just inside the doorway looking up at the ceiling.

"This is marvelous; it looks so real. But where is it coming from?"

Eleanor snuck up behind Charles and put a handful of snow down his shirt. She doubled over in tears laughing at him as he danced around in a circle trying to get it out.

Lucas and Tiffany were by the fireplace, where she formed snowballs behind him as he threw them.

Charlie used the sectional as a shield, ducking behind it as he formed an impressive pile of ammunition. He popped up and threw them aimlessly in all directions as he dove back down for cover.

Caleb slipped and faceplanted in a mound of snow. Laughing,

Emily extended her hand. He gave her a wicked grin and gently pulled her into the snow with him.

Natalie, still a little shy around the family, paused in the doorway, smiling as she watched her husband act like a giant man-child. Unable to resist the fun, she crouched behind the sectional next to Charlie and began forming snowballs for him since he had already gone through more than half of his original pile.

Luna and Ben joined in, helping the kids take down all the other adults. After hours of playing in the snow, it was unanimously decided that they would get cleaned up and have some hot cocoa. Luna prayed that ten people would be too big of an order and the library would mind its own business.

When it was just her and Ben left in the room, she asked, "Where did you hide it?"

Ben approached *Expand Your Home*'s display stand and pulled a book from behind it.

"You are brilliant." Luna beamed and kissed him.

"I know," he said, closing the book, and with it, clearing the snow and setting the library back to normal.

The parlor and hallway were a jumble of bodies as they hugged and said their goodbyes.

Stopping at the front door, Emily said, "Don't forget to send me the brand of instant snow you use for the kids."

Before a frowning Luna could respond, Tiffany tugged on her mother's coat sleeve and said, "It's magic."

Emily nodded and winked. "Okay."

As they walked down the steps, Lucas asked his parents if they could get a library at their house. Luna smiled and shook her head.

"Goodbye, dear," Eleanor said, pulling Luna in for a hug.

"Bye, Mom."

"You know, this was probably in the top five for best Larson and Millbrook Icicle Inn-Cursions. I am getting up there in age, so maybe we should have more of them here. Who knows? Maybe the next one will be a Larson, Millbrook, and Lattimore event." She winked at Ben.

"Mom, was that a compliment?" Luna opened her mouth and put her hand on her chest, feigning shock.

With the last guest out of the house, Luna shut the door and took a deep breath. Ben grabbed her hand and led her through the open door into the library, where a plate of chocolate chip cookies and a bowl of popcorn along with a thick hunter-green book with gold foil lettering waited for them on the table in front of the gray loveseat.

The fireplace roared to life as they snuggled under the maroon, wool blanket and Ben fed Luna snacks as she read aloud.

"Did you hear that?" Ben whispered.

"Hear what?"

"Nothing. We have the house all to ourselves." He smiled.

Luna picked up a handful of popcorn and tossed it at Ben. "If the silence bothers you, we can always call them back."

As Ben opened his mouth to speak, the library door slammed shut and the lock clicked into place.

They looked at each other and laughed.

About the Author

S.B. Rizk lives in Medford, Massachusetts with her husband and their two sons. In her free time she loves to draw, cook and read. She has an extensive background in culinary arts, but her true passion has always been with books. Most of her teenage years were spent inside, with her nose in a book. As an adult she spends as much time weaving her own stories as she does reading others.

Connect with her on Instagram to check out her latest projects and to see what other bookish things she is up to. Or visit her Linktree to find direct links to her website and books.

You can find S.B. Rizk on:
Instagram @author.sarahrizk

And visit her website at linktr.ee/author.sarahrizk

Contributor Library

Please also look for these titles, which were authored by, published by, or feature the authors in this anthology.

Autumn 2024 Anthology
Querencia Press
Guihan Larsen

Bad Idea Lane
A Novel
Krista Renee

Beautiful
The Fragile Line, Book 1
Sarah Dawson Powell

May I Have Your Attention Please
McKinney High Class of 1986, Book 1
Debby Meltzer Quick

Don't Say a Word
Anomaly, Book 1
Debby Meltzer Quick

About the Editor

Nicole Frail has been editing fiction and nonfiction books for adults and children for fifteen years. Between 2012 and 2024, she worked as an acquisitions and project editor for a traditional publisher based in New York City while simultaneously working with independent/self-publishing authors via her small business, Nicole Frail Edits.

In mid-2024, she switched gears and decided to take her "side gig" full time, expanding the services offered through Nicole Frail Edits, LLC. Shortly after, she formed her own small press, Nicole Frail Books, LLC, to publish anthologies born out of short story contests as well as ebooks and other projects still to come.

Nicole lives just outside Scranton, Pennsylvania, with her husband, three little boys, and two Tuxedo cats.

You can find Nicole Frail on:
Instagram @nicolefrailedits & @nicolefrailbooks
Facebook @nicolefrailedits & @nicolefrailbooks

And visit her websites at www.nicolefrailedits.com
& www.nicolefrailbooks.com

Acknowledgments

This itty-bitty publishing house may be a one-woman operation on paper, but it is, by no means, a one-woman show behind the scenes.

To start, I'd like to send a big thank-you to the authors in this anthology who enthusiastically agreed to go down this path with me—and stayed on it while I figured out how to balance two businesses, three kids, two cats, and one husband . . . and somehow remain sane. (Spoiler alert: I haven't figured this out yet. Anyone have tips? I'll take them!)

If you're unfamiliar, *As the Snow Drifts* is the first release from And You Press, an imprint of Nicole Frail Books, LLC, so despite previous publishing house experience, this book (and the second—I'm not forgetting about you, *Another Chance to Get It Right*!) is the start of a brand-new experience for me. And it's certainly shining the light on everything I know versus everything I don't know . . . versus everything I thought I knew about book publishing.

And that is why, authors of this anthology, your support, feedback, praise, and excitement over everything related to this collection kept me going on the days imposter syndrome crept in, and for that, I am so incredibly grateful. Thank you, thank you, thank you.

I'd also like to extend my thanks to—

My sister, Kerri Odell, for the beautiful cover and interior elements. You are appreciated, and I should say it more.

My first reader, Elizabeth Cunningham, who helped me select the winners of the contest this summer.

My final reader, Bernadette Frail (Mom!), who pitched in at the eleventh hour when I needed a fresh set of eyes.

My interns from Wilkes University, Sydney Ahrberg and Shawn Carey, who assisted me in putting together this collection.

Plunge Into Books Tours, for their aid in marketing/tour management.

Members of the NFB Street Team, for their enthusiasm and support.

And finally, my husband, Matthew, and our three boys—Cooper, Travis, and Eli. Thank you for every big hug and sweet kiss. You're my whole world.

Milton Keynes UK
Ingram Content Group UK Ltd.
UKHW030848141124
451205UK00005B/399